THE EVOLUTION OF FREUD

THE EVOLUTION OF FREUD
His Theoretical Development of the Mind–Body Relationship and the Role of Sexuality

Barry R. Silverstein

PHOENIX
PUBLISHING HOUSE
firing the mind

First published in 2022 by
Phoenix Publishing House Ltd
62 Bucknell Road
Bicester
Oxfordshire OX26 2DS

British Library Cataloguing in Publication Data

A C.I.P. for this book is available from the British Library

ISBN-13: 978-1-912691-40-1

Typeset by Medlar Publishing Solutions Pvt Ltd, India

www.firingthemind.com

*For
Lorraine,
Steven, and Judy*

Contents

Part II
Freud on sexuality and neuroses

Acknowledgments

First and foremost, I express my gratitude and appreciation to my partner, Lorraine Lener-Ciancio, who makes all things possible. Her support and technical-editorial assistance made this book a reality. Thanks to Dr. Steven M. Silverstein who offered helpful comments on a draft of Part I, and to Professor Brett Kahr for his early encouragement to expand an essay into a book. Many thanks to David Joseph for always sending me books on Freud he thinks I should read. Appreciation to James Darley for thoughtful and thorough editing. And last but not least, thanks to Kate Pearce of Phoenix Publishing House, for believing in this work and seeing it through to fruition.

About the author

Barry R. Silverstein is emeritus professor in the Department of Psychology, William Paterson University, Wayne, NJ. His early research as a developmental psychologist produced the book (with Ronald Krate) *Children of the Dark Ghetto: A Developmental Psychology* (Praeger, 1975), a study of the development of minority, inner-city children that is still widely cited. As an independent Freud researcher for more than forty years he has published on the history of psychoanalysis in the journals: *The Psychoanalytic Review, American Imago, The Annual of Psychoanalysis, American Psychologist, Psych CRITIQUES, The Journal of Psychohistory*, and *Psychological Reports*. His Freud studies essays have been published in the volumes: *Freud: Appraisals and Reappraisals: Contributions to Freud Studies, Vol. 1* (The Analytic Press, 1986), and *Sigmund Freud: Critical Assessments* (Routledge, 1989). His invited essay on the origins and history of psychoanalysis was published in *The Freud Encyclopedia Encyclopedia: Theory, Therapy, and Culture* (Routledge, 2002). He authored the book: *What was Freud Thinking? A Short Historical Introduction to Freud's Theories and Therapies* (Kendall-Hunt, 2003). He was a frequently invited reviewer for the journal *Psychoanalytic Books*.

Foreword

by Brett Kahr

To the very best of our knowledge, no human being has ever worked harder than Sigmund Freud.

The father of psychoanalysis would awaken not long after 7.00 a.m. each morning and would then toil continuously throughout the day, treating patient after patient, writing book after book, and tending to his extensive international correspondence until the small hours of the morning. He devoted so much time to the advancement of the psychological profession that if he had lived today in the twenty-first century, he would undoubtedly have developed either repetitive strain injury in his wrists or forward head posture syndrome from having chained himself to his home computer for too many hours, replying to untold numbers of text messages and e-mails!

In view of Freud's extraordinary productivity, we have no shortage of amazing monographs, essays, and letters—literally thousands upon thousands of documents—produced by this incredible genius, all of which contributed to the creation of an unparalleled paradigm shift in the understanding and treatment of the human mind.

But studying the prolific—indeed seemingly never-ending—*oeuvre* of Sigmund Freud properly does require a tremendous investment of time and energy; and, alas, most people today—including many fellow psychoanalytical practitioners—have neglected to engage with the breadth and detail of Freud's unique library of contributions.

Thankfully, Professor Barry Silverstein, a psychologist and Freud scholar of long standing, has generously crafted a concise and readable and accurate text which truly explains and embraces many of the great achievements of Sigmund Freud in a most engaging and inspiring style. In this very digestible book, Silverstein has treated us to what he has described, quite correctly, as a "guided tour."

Not only has Silverstein escorted us on a guided tour but he has dared to tackle some of the most challenging and theoretically complex areas of Freud's theories, which require great intellectual rigor, not least when immersing oneself in a detailed examination of Freud's observations about the seemingly unsolvable "mind–body" dilemma as well as his engagement with the etiology of the neuroses and other psychological states, including the causal role of sexuality.

In my estimation, Silverstein's book, *The Evolution of Freud: His Theoretical Development of the Mind–Body Relationship and the Role of Sexuality*, may well be one of the very best means of encountering Freud and engaging with his life and work. Moreover, this text will be of value not only to new students but, also, to old friends as well, as each of us still has so very much to learn about the progenitor of modern global mental health.

I congratulate Professor Silverstein on this outstanding and, indeed, loving achievement, and I recommend this book most warmly to us all.

Professor Brett Kahr
Senior Fellow, Tavistock Institute of Medical Psychology, London
Honorary Director of Research, Freud Museum, London

Preface

The narrative and text presented in this book will place the development of some of Sigmund Freud's work in historical context. As Freud himself stated:

> Psycho-Analysis may be said to have been born with the twentieth century .... But, as may well be supposed, it did not drop from the skies ready-made. It had its starting-point in older ideas, which it developed further; it sprang from earlier suggestions, which it elaborated. Any history of it must therefore begin with an account of the influences which determined its origin, and should not overlook the times and circumstances that preceded its creation.
>
> (Freud, 1924f, p. 191)

This book has two main focal points: the development of Freud's thinking concerning the relationship between mind and body, and his ideas concerning the role of sexuality in human development, behavior, and the creation of neurotic disturbances. We will follow the inner movement of Freud's thinking, its meaning and coherence, as well as his conceptual logic and personal directions. I have attempted to locate the development of Freud's thinking within the context of the intellectual, medical, scientific, and cultural currents swirling around him. A concern is how the changing circumstances of his personal life, particularly his sexual life, and his personalized professional rivalries, stimulated his thinking about the role of sexuality in human motivation, development, and the creation of adult neuroses.

To follow Freud's path as he developed his theories, I have let him speak for himself by utilizing his own words on how he formulated the crucial points that became the building blocks of his system—a guided tour of his original foundational writing, published and unpublished.

Part I provides a detailed study of Freud's mind–body views. It traces his development of a pragmatic dualist-interactionist approach that maintained a critical distinction between the material body and the mental subjective world. He focused on what went on within the mind in relation to the necessity to reduce tensions (feelings) subjectively experienced within the lived-in body, caused by physiological changes in the material body. He concentrated on a particular link between mental processes and the organic substrate: sexual physiology.

Part II focuses on Freud's evolving views on the role of sexuality in the causation of neuroses and his differentiation of particular neuroses based upon varying specific underlying sexual causes. We will follow his changing attempts to develop therapeutic tactics to bring cures to his patients, as well as the trajectory of his changing views on the role of deferred action of childhood experiences as prerequisites for adult neuroses, the development of childhood sexuality (as rooted in evolutionary biology), and the role of different childhood experiences that produce adult character types connected to differentiated adult psychoneurotic symptoms.

Part I

Freud on mind and body

Introduction

Part I explores Freud's confrontation with the mind–body relationship. His early clinical work presented him with a number of puzzling questions: Using hypnosis, how can spoken words (ideas) cause physical changes in a patient's body (see Silverstein & Silverstein, 1990), and how can hysterical patients' self-generated ideas concerning their bodies, particularly thoughts rooted in sexuality, produce physical symptoms (see Silverstein, 1985, 2003)? In facing these conundrums, Freud did not function as a detached philosopher, he created explanatory theories that made sense to him based upon his own experiences with the clinical material he had at hand.

We will review how certain significant mentors and role models in his education and early clinical experience moved Freud to believe that not only should mind (thoughts, ideas) be distinguished from the physical body (brain) within a dualistic-interactionist conceptual paradigm, but also that psychical processes have some independent power and efficacy to produce effects in the physical body. We will follow Freud's construction and sequential reconstructions of his metapsychology— conceptions of the nature, dynamics, and principles of unconscious mental functioning and changing concepts of the nature and purpose of dreams. In addition, we will examine his motivational concepts of inherent human conflicts rooted in instinctual drives (a mind–body connection) and how conflicts with sexuality lead to ego defenses that determine healthy versus neurotic development and behavior.

CHAPTER 1

Mind and body

In considering what distinguished mind from body, Freud had been greatly influenced early on by his philosophy professor, Franz Brentano who taught that it was necessary to distinguish between psychical or mental processes and physical-physiological processes. Mental phenomena represented a distinct phenomenal realm, subjective reality, with distinctive properties not found in the material world. Brentano (1874) defined mental phenomena as "those phenomena which contain an object intentionally within themselves ... No physical phenomenon exhibits anything like it" (p. 89). Motivational factors—subjective intentionality—were extremely important in determining the flow of thought. What was mental had to be understood in terms appropriate to the quality of subjective reality; the mental world could not be equated with, or reduced to, a physiological substrate (see Brentano, 1874, pp. 63–64).

Brentano (1874) argued that

> the relationship between mental phenomena and concomitant physiological phenomena is actually very different from that which exists between the inorganic phenomena with which

the chemist deals and the organisms with which the physiologist deals ... the difference between physiological processes and chemical and physical processes really seems to be only that physiological processes are more complex ... the more comprehensive concept of chemical phenomena has been shown to apply uniformly to inorganic changes and to life in the physiological sense. We can hardly say the same thing ... when we apply it to the physiological and psychological realms ... if we turn our attention from the external world to the inner, we find ourselves, as it were, in a new realm. The phenomena are absolutely heterogeneous ... It was for that very reason that we separated the psychological and physical sciences as the main branches of empirical science ... (pp. 50–51)

Further,

Not only the surrender of psychological investigation to physiological research, but also the mixing of the latter with the former seems by and large ill-advised in important areas. At the moment there are only a very few established physiological facts of the sort which could shed light upon mental phenomena. (p. 64)

Brentano taught Freud that an empirical scientist should not limit himself to a one-sided materialism in thinking about mind and body. One could be both scientific and empirical while taking a two-sided approach, one which avoided a strictly physicalistic and reductionistic stance. (See Silverstein, 1985; McGrath, 1986; Cohen, 2002; Whitebook, 2017; Bergo, 2018.)

The influence was so strong that, when he was still a student of Brentano in 1875, Freud characterized himself as "a former swashbuckling stubborn materialist," even though he felt uncomfortable abandoning previously held faith in what was generally held to be correct, and he was trying to keep an open mind (in Boehlich, 1990, p. 109). Between 1874 and 1876, Freud took five courses with Brentano (Merlan, 1949). These were the only nonscience courses Freud took at the University of Vienna Medical School, and not one of these was a course which Freud was required to take (Jones, 1953, p. 37).

For six years, between 1876 and 1882, Freud worked in Ernst Brücke's physiological laboratory carrying out histological research, microscopic studies on the structure of the cells of the nervous system (see Solms, 2002). Freud greatly admired Brücke as a teacher and mentor. Brücke and Emil Du Bois-Reymond were pioneers in the development of an understanding of the mechanisms of physical forces in physiological processes. They also were longtime associates. They both believed that physiological processes had to be understood as the lawful expression of physical and chemical forces at work in the body. In 1842, Du Bois-Reymond had written to a friend:

> Brücke and I pledged a solemn oath to put in power this truth: No other forces than the common physical chemical ones are active within the organism. In those cases which cannot at the time be explained by these forces one has either to find the specific way or form of their action by means of the physical mathematical method, or to assume new forces equal in dignity to the chemical physical forces inherent in matter, reducible to the force of attraction and repulsion. (Quoted in Bernfeld, 1944, p. 348)

Although the quote is accurate, Cranefield (1970, pp. 47–48) corrects an error in Bernfeld's citation. This often-quoted youthful oath was a rebellion against the then-current belief in a unique vital force found only in living organisms. However, Brücke's and Du Bois-Reymond's oath applied to the explanation of physiological phenomena. It was not addressed to an understanding of mental phenomena or the relationship between mind and matter. From the work of Brücke and Du Bois-Reymond Freud was influenced to expect lawful, deterministic, energic forces to operate in mental phenomena as they did in physical phenomena, but neither Brücke nor Du Bois-Reymond advocated the reduction of higher-level mental processes to the exact physical and chemical forces at work in the body (see Cranefield, 1966a, 1966b, and Gregory, 1977, pp. 145–163).

Freud greatly admired the eminent physiologist Du Bois-Reymond. In January 1875, Freud told a friend that if he could have financed the project, he had hoped to spend the 1875–76 winter semester in Berlin, in part, to attend the lectures of Du Bois-Reymond (in Boehlich, 1990, p. 84). In a March 1875 letter, Freud made reference to his familiarity with Du Bois-Reymond's famous 1872 lecture entitled, *On the Limits of our Understanding of Nature,* when he made reference to "the dubois-Reymond limits of cognition" (in Boehlich, 1990, p. 107). Thirty years after his youthful 1842 oath with Brücke, even though he rigorously defended the truth of a mechanistic account of the world, Du Bois-Reymond argued that there were certain limits beyond which scientific understanding could not go. Faced with the questions how are nerve processes related to conscious experience and what is the relationship between nerve processes and the qualities to which they give rise, Du Bois-Reymond (1872) stated that he would have to say, "ignorabimus," we will not be able to know; we will ignore it (p. 464). Further, Du Bois-Reymond (1872) stated:

> The more unconditionally the natural science researcher recognizes and accepts the limits set for him, and the more humbly he resigns himself to his ignorance, the more strongly he feels it is his right to come to his own opinion about the relationship between mind and matter, by way of his own induction, unmoved along the way by myths, dogmas and proud old philosophers. (Original German text Du Bois-Reymond, 1872, pp. 460–461, as translated in Silverstein (2002, p. 439))

Mindful of Brentano's views and Du Bois-Reymond's warning that there might be limits to human understanding, Freud adopted and maintained a skepticism toward any uniting of the mental and the physical into an all-embracing materialistic monism. He was fond of quoting the poet Heine's derisive comment on metaphysical philosophers who cling to the illusion of being able to present a coherent picture of the universe without any gaps: "With his nightcaps and the tatters of his dressing-gown, he patches up the gaps in the structure of the universe" (see Freud, 1933a, pp. 160–161).

Consistent with Du Bois-Reymond's "ignorabimus" stance concerning the relationship between neurophysiological processes and the existence of consciousness, Freud accepted that consciousness was an enigma whose existence could not be explained by reference to neuroanatomy or neurophysiology. Early in his career in an article entitled "The Brain" (*Gehirn*) prepared for Villaret's 1888 encyclopedic *Handbook of Medicine*, Freud stated that although there was a lawful connection between changes in the material brain and changes in the conscious mind, he could not understand the nature of the connection between brain and mind. Freud (1888) stated:

> Although the mechanical process is not understood, it is the actual presence of this coupling of material changes of conditions in the brain with changes in the state of the conscious mind which makes the brain a center of psychic activity. Although the essence of this coupling is incomprehensible to us, it is not haphazard, and on the basis of combinations of experiences of the outer senses on the one hand and inner-perception on the other we can determine something about the laws which govern this coupling. (Original German text 1888, p. 691, as translated in Silverstein, 1985, p. 209)

A full translation of *Gehirn* (1888) may be found in Solms and Saling (1990, pp. 39–86). At the end of his career, in *An Outline of Psycho-Analysis*, Freud (1940a) essentially repeated his 1888 statement:

> We note two kinds of things about what we call our psyche (or mental life); firstly it's bodily organ and scene of action, the brain (or nervous system) and, on the other hand, our acts of consciousness, which are immediate data and cannot be further explained by any sort of description. Everything that lies between is unknown to us, and the data do not include any direct relation between these two terminal points of our knowledge. (p. 144)

Concerning what lay between the material brain and conscious experience, in 1888 at the start of his career when he was trying to understand symptom formation in his hysterical patients, Freud conceptualized the existence of unobservable mental processes that were not part of ordinary consciousness, but that, nevertheless, could affect the functions of the material body. Freud (1888b) argued that

> the psychical changes which must be postulated as being the foundation of the hysterical *status* take place wholly in the sphere of unconscious, automatic, cerebral activity. It may, perhaps, further be emphasized that in hysteria the influence of psychical processes on physical processes in the organism (as in all neuroses) is increased ... (p. 49)

Following Charcot, with whom he studied in Paris from late 1885 to early 1886 (Freud, 1893f), Freud believed that it was ideas (patients' *thoughts*) concerning parts of their body outside ordinary conscious awareness or control that had the power to *realize themselves objectively* in shaping the nature of *physical representations* in hysteria. He was not viewing unconscious psychical processes as identical with concomitant physical brain processes; they were qualitatively different variables that interacted in ways that Freud believed were lawful, in spite of the fact that their mode of coupling remained incomprehensible to him.

In arguing for the role of mind–body interaction in the causation of hysteria, Freud (1888b) stated that an

> extremely important characteristic of hysterical disorders is that they do not in any way present a copy of the anatomical conditions of the nervous system. It may be said that hysteria is as ignorant of the science of the structure of the nervous system as we ourselves before we have learnt it. (pp. 48–49)

Continuing with this theme later, Freud (1893c) explicitly argued for the role of ideas in causing hysterical paralyses. He pointed out that hysterical paralyses conformed to the patient's images of anatomy, not to anatomical facts: "the lesion in hysterical paralyses must be completely independent of the anatomy of the nervous system, since *in its paralyses and other manifestations hysteria behaves as though anatomy did not exist or as though it had no knowledge of it*" (p. 169, Freud's italics).

By the time Freud wrote his 1891 neurological monograph, *On Aphasia*, it is clear that he also had been influenced by the British neurologist, John Hughlings Jackson (see Freud 1891b, pp. 54–66). Hughlings Jackson had insisted that it was a pragmatic methodological necessity for neurologists to treat the mental and the physical as distinctly different phenomena. They were knowable by different methods, and required distinct, separate mentalistic and physicalistic modes of description and explanation. "It is impossible to study cases of diseases of the brain methodically if we confuse psychical states with nervous states" (Hughlings Jackson, 1881, p. 9). "There is no physiology of the mind any more than there is psychology of the nervous system," he insisted (Hughlings Jackson, 1890, p. 417). Similarly, Freud (1891b) questioned: "Is it justified to immerse a nerve fiber, which over the whole length of its course has been only a physiological structure subject to physiological modifications, with its end in the psyche, and to furnish this end with an idea or a memory?" (p. 55).

Hughlings Jackson assumed a parallelism, or concomitance, between mental states and conditions of the nervous system. However, his parallelism was not strictly an ontological position that was a definition of the mind–brain relationship. Rather, he saw psychophysical parallelism as a pragmatic position from which to advance the study of the brain. Hughlings Jackson wished to avoid getting caught up in unanswerable metaphysical questions raised by a mind–body interactionist position, and he wished to avoid attributing mental properties to neurological states. In 1875 he stated: "We cannot understand how any conceivable arrangement of any sort of matter can give us mental states of any kind … I do not trouble myself about the mode of connection between mind and matter. It is enough to assume a parallelism" (p. 52). Further, he argued, "I then ask that the doctrine of concomitance be provisionally accepted as an artifice, in order that we may study the most complex diseases of the nervous system more easily" (1887, p. 85). While Freud might use the two-sided artifice of psychophysical parallelism when considering certain conditions caused by neurological damage, such as aphasia, his observations of the effects of hypnotic suggestion on the body and his psychogenic approach to hysteria required Freud to go beyond the artifice of psychophysical parallelism: When it came to hysteria, he had to assume that some sort of interaction between the mental and physical realms occurred in this affliction. (See Silverstein, 1985; Meissner, 2003; Bergo, 2018.)

Hughlings Jackson believed that neurologists had to turn to psychology in order to understand the rules, or organizing principles, of the ideational and linguistic accompaniments of complex nervous activities. He proposed an evolutionary, hierarchical model of the nervous system and of mental functioning with lower-level mental functioning dominated by a prelinguistic mode of cognition, which followed rules of association different from those found in higher-level, linguistically organized mental processes. Freud incorporated Hughlings Jackson's ideas in his evolving conceptions of the dynamics of neuroses, and in his evolving topographical theory of mental functioning, to be discussed below, which he first published in *The Interpretation of Dreams* (1900a). For some commentaries on Hughlings Jackson's influence on Freud, see Forrester (1980, pp. 1–62); Fullinwider (1983); Solms and Saling (1986); Harrington (1987, pp. 235–247); Goldstein (1995); Sacks (1998).

In the early 1880s, Theodor Meynert, Freud's professor of nervous diseases in Vienna, had offered Freud a place in his laboratory to conduct neuroanatomical research. Freud was conducting brain anatomy research in Meynert's laboratory in 1885 when Meynert published his textbook, *Psychiatry* (see Solms, 2002). Meynert (1885, pp. 246–248) argued that consciousness was a function of the level of nervous excitation associated with residual cortical images; those images which acquired the prerequisite high level of nervous excitation automatically rose above the threshold of consciousness. However, by the start of the 1890s, influenced by Hughlings Jackson, contrary to Meynert, Freud adopted the idea that a translation, or recategorization, from lower-level prelinguistic modes of thinking in images into linguistic modes of representation was necessary for mentation below the threshold of consciousness to become and remain fully conscious. Freud would go on to describe the emergence of consciousness as a progressive process of differentiation: "It is probable that thinking was originally unconscious insofar as it went beyond mere ideational presentations and was directed to the relations between impressions of objects, and that it did not acquire further qualities, perceptible to consciousness, until it became connected with verbal residues" (Freud, 1911b, p. 221). The possibility of a failure to translate unconscious images into the linguistic categories required for consciousness became a fundamental premise behind Freud's concept of primal repression, and the distinctions between primary and secondary process mental functions as discussed below.

Freud focused on sexuality as a two-sided phenomenon which linked the subjectively knowable mental world and the empirically knowable physical world. He saw apparent connections between sexuality in the mental realm—sexual thoughts and intentions, and sexuality in the physical realm—changes in physiology and internal excitation of the nervous system. Basing his reasoning upon such considerations, Freud adopted a pragmatic-dualistic-interactionist position on the mind–body relationship: the mental world had to be observed through inner perception and described in motivational-intentional language, while the physical world was observed empirically, and described in terms from physics and chemistry. Nevertheless, he believed that the mental and the physical interacted in that ideas could produce effects in the body, while changes in physiology could affect motivation and thought. In 1890, Freud specifically argued for the existence of mind–body interaction when he declared:

> The relationship between body and mind … is a reciprocal one; but in earlier times the other side of this relation, the effect of the mind upon the body found little favour in the eyes of physicians. They seemed to be afraid of granting mental life any independence, for fear of that implying an abandonment of the scientific ground on which they stood. (1890a, p. 284)

Furthermore, concerning neurotic patients, Freud (1890a) argued that "in some at least of these patients the signs of their illness originate from nothing other than *a change in the action of their minds upon their bodies* …" (p. 286, Freud's italics). He went on to point out that mental activities could produce such physical consequences as changes in heart-action and alterations in the distribution of blood in the body (p. 287). Freud may have been influenced to think about psychosomatic affects by his reading of Tuke's (1884) *Illustrations of the Influence of the Mind upon the Body in Health and Disease*. He underlined many passages in his copy of this volume (Eissler, 2001, p. 360, n.). Remaining consistent in his mind–body interaction views, at the end of his career, Freud continued to argue: "psychical phenomena are to a high degree dependent upon somatic influences and on their side have the most powerful effects upon somatic processes" (1940b, p. 283).

Even though the mechanism(s) that governed mind–body interaction remained unknown to Freud, he avoided a reductionistic position. He created a theory of mind which incorporated two fundamentally different classes of phenomena: the mental and the physical (see Silverstein, 1985, 1988, 1989a, 2002, 2003; Silverstein & Silverstein, 1990, and Parisi, 1987). Freud not only asserted that ideas possessed causal efficacy, but it was unconscious ideas following their own associational rules, not discoverable by simple introspection, which most powerfully affected bodily functions. Nevertheless, Freud accepted the view that the puzzling leap from the mental to the physical was inexplicable. According to Freud (1909d) "the leap from a mental process to a somatic innervation … can never be fully comprehensible to us" (p. 157). Nevertheless, he remained profoundly influenced by his teacher Charcot's dictum concerning materialist orthodoxy, which left "an indelible mark" upon his mind: "Theory is good; but it doesn't prevent things from existing" (Freud, 1893f, p. 13).

By the time he completed *The Interpretation of Dreams* in the year 1899, Freud believed that most mental processes were in themselves unconscious and that consciousness itself was determined by unconscious mental processes. Unconscious mental processes were intentional, and their motivational impetus originated within the body. In neurosis, the underlying organic factor was to be found in the motivational excitation resulting from sexual physiology (see Silverstein, 1985, 2003; Hughes, 1994; Sugarman, 2016). In fact, in 1908, Freud insisted to C. G. Jung: "In the sexual processes we have the indispensable 'organic foundation' without which a medical man can only feel ill at ease in the life of the psyche" (in McGuire, 1974, pp. 140–141). These lines of thinking were the basis for Freud's topographical theory of mental functioning and his motivational theory of instinctual drives, both of which will be discussed below.

In 1908, Freud told Jung that he had "absolutely foresworn the temptation to 'fill in the gaps in the universe'" (in McGuire, 1974, p. 125). Writing to Josef Popper-Lynkeus in 1916, Freud argued: "No doubt the Uncs. is the right mediator between the physical and the mental, perhaps it is the long-sought for 'missing link'" (in E. L. Freud, 1961, p. 324). Freud accused Popper-Lynkeus, the philosopher, of having the monistic tendency to disparage the difference between psychological and physical phenomena in favor of tempting unity. "But," Freud insisted, "does this help to eliminate the differences?" (p. 324). Stressing the need to differentiate what was mental (psychical) from what was physical (echoing Brentano), Freud told the Vienna Psychoanalytic Society in 1912: "If the present speaker had to choose among the views of the philosophers, he could characterize himself as a dualist. No monism succeeds in doing away with the distinction between ideas and the objects they represent" (in Nunberg & Federn, 1975, vol. 4, p. 136).

CHAPTER 2

From "The Project" to metapsychology

In *Studies on Hysteria* (1895d), Freud argued that memories were excluded from consciousness and became pathogenic as a result of the patient being in conflict with the content of the memories. Such conflict arose because the memory content was incompatible with the patient's conscious view of self. The patient intentionally repressed or excluded from consciousness ideas that were incompatible with a positive conscious self-image, a psychical act of self-defense. According to Freud, "we have been led to the view that hysteria originates through the repression of an incompatible idea from a motive of defence" (Freud & Breuer, 1895d, p. 285). The previous year, Freud had stated: "In hysteria, the incompatible idea is rendered innocuous by its *sum of excitation being transformed into something somatic*. For this I should like to propose the name of *conversion*" (1894, p. 49, Freud's italics).

For Freud in 1895, hysteria and psychic conflict over pathogenic memories involved defense and compromise formation. Excitation associated with an incompatible idea embedded in a repressed memory was channeled into a somatic innervation that produced a physical symptom. This physical symptom was a compromise formation in that it now occupied a patient's consciousness in place of the incompatible idea which it symbolically represented in a manner not consciously recognized—a poetic use of the body to represent, metaphorically, an unacceptable idea concerning one's self. For example: A self-threatening repressed memory associated with a romantic rejection which was "*like a slap in the face*" might be represented physically as experienced facial pain with a facial tic; a self-threatening repressed memory associated with unrequited love and the thought, "*I can't stand it*" might be represented physically as experienced paralysis of the legs; a self-threatening repressed memory associated with a perceived betrayal and the thought, "*I have been stabbed in the heart*" might be represented physically as experienced pain in the chest. During the early 1890s, Freud increasingly suspected that the sum of excitation, the energy misdirected into the nervous system that was converted into a hysterical symptom, was sexual excitation that had been aroused in association with an incompatible repressed idea. The psychological thrust of Freud's early approach to neuroses during the 1890s has been explored at length by Andersson (1962), Stewart (1967), Levin (1978), and May (1999).

Freud had been unhappy with Breuer's theory chapter in their joint publication, *Studies on Hysteria* (1895d). While he shared with Breuer a physiological emphasis on an economics of the nerve-force as a necessary part of an explanation of hysteria, he wanted an explanatory model that also could accommodate his evolving explanatory emphases on intentions, conflicts, defense, and compromise in hysterical symptom formation. Freud struggled to create a mechanistic model that would be superior to the one he found in Breuer's theory chapter.

On May 25, 1895, Freud told Wilhelm Fliess that "a satisfactory general conception of neuropsychotic disturbances is impossible if one cannot link it with clear assumptions about normal mental processes" (in Masson, 1985, p. 129). Furthermore, Freud declared: "I am tormented by two aims: to examine what shape the theory of mental functioning takes if one introduces quantitative considerations, a sort of economics of nerve forces; and second, to peel off from psychopathology a gain for normal psychology" (in Masson, 1985, p. 129).

Freud already had expressed a quantitative working hypothesis at the conclusion of his 1894 paper, *The Neuro-Psychoses of Defence*. Here, Freud explained that such reasoning helped him to organize his clinical data:

> I refer to the concept that in mental functions something is to
> be distinguished—a quota of affect or sum of excitation—which
> possesses all the characteristics of a quantity (though we have
> no means of measuring it), which is capable of increase, dimi-
> nution, displacement and discharge, and which is spread over
> the memory—traces of ideas somewhat as an electric charge is
> spread over the surface of a body. (p. 60)

This hypothesis already underlay the theory that hysterics needed to discharge energy, originally associated with excessively intense trau-matic memories, which Breuer and Freud had put forth in their 1893 preliminary communication, and which they stated again in 1895 in *Studies on Hysteria*.

On April 27, 1895 Freud told Fliess that he was working on a proj-ect he referred to as: *The Psychology for Neurologists* (not "Neurology for Psychologists"). After returning home from a visit with Fliess in September 1895, Freud told him that he was writing an account of his psychology for him to criticize (in Masson, 1985, p. 139). About two weeks later, Freud mailed two notebooks to him which contained an elaborate mechanis-tic model which he hoped would be a more rigorous, comprehensive, precise theoretical model—to explain the excessively intense ideas and psychical defenses found in hysteria and obsessional neurosis—than the mechanical physiological explanation for hysteria supplied by Breuer. These notebooks which Freud never published have become known as the "Project for a Scientific Psychology" (Freud, 1950a).

Freud introduced the Project by stating that it was his intention "to furnish a psychology that shall be a natural science" (p. 295). Writing in German, Freud used the words, "*eine naturwissenschaftliche Psychologie*" to refer to psychology as a natural science. The term *wissenschaftliche* is based upon the German word *Wissenschaft* that might be translated into English as "science." However, while it might be translated as science, the German word had a much broader meaning for Freud than in the limited positivist sense of experimental or laboratory science. In the late nine-teenth-century German university system, any product of critical schol-arship that contributed to the advancement of human knowledge could be included under the broad umbrella of *Wissenschaften*. Thus archeol-ogy, sociology, psychology, economics, even biblical criticism, would be

Wissenschaften when studied according to certain standards of acceptable scholarship (D. B. Klein, 1970, p. 761n., 817). However, the German university system of the late nineteenth century distinguished between two categories of *Wissenschaften* respectively: *Naturwissenschaften*, the natural sciences, and *Geisteswissenschaften*, the human sciences (see Bettelheim, 1983, pp. 40–49). Natural sciences, such as physics, studied the machine that is the universe from an external perspective seeking the laws that determined natural events. *Naturwissenschaften* sought to find the *causes* of natural events: causes were conceptualized as forms of matter set in motion by unobservable energetic forces that followed Newtonian laws. *Geisteswissenschaften*, or human sciences such as history, used a first-person perspective seeking to find *reasons* for human events viewed from the inside and conceptualized as intentions, goals, and meanings.

Even though Freud conceived his Project as part of *Naturwissenschaften*, and even though he began the Project by *representing* different *mental processes* as if they were the mechanical accompaniments of a set of hypothetical, functionally differentiated, neuronal structures that were "specifiable material particles," and he accounted for psychical activity in terms of quantities of energy distributed among hypothetical neuronal systems "subject to the general laws of motion" (1950a, p. 295), Freud was not trying to reduce *psychology* to materialistic neurology; what he was *representing* was qualitatively different *mental* phenomena as connected to the functions of conceptual neuronal systems. He knew there were no then-available histological or neurological facts to support the existence of his specific functionally differentiated conceptual neurons (see Amacher, 1965, p. 65), although his theorizing that his hypothetical neurons communicated with each other through transferring energy across "contact barriers" did have a precedent in Ramón y Cajal's 1888 proposal of neuronal communication across separating zones of contact between them (see Sotelo, 2020). The neurons of Freud's Project were his inventions to try to explain clinical data based upon references to entities and forces mechanically determining mental life (Kanzer, 1973, p. 91). In this light the Project is best viewed as a clinical psychology text in which "Freud's psychology is not so much an economics of *neurons*, but rather an economics of *ideas*" (Geerardyn, 1997, pp. 221–222). His neurons "were just made-up pseudo-scientific names for psychological functions" (Makari, 2008, p. 73). The Project was Freud's attempt to build a systematic model of mental functions—his *Psychology for Neurologists*—within the limits imposed by a mechanistic *Naturwissenschaften* paradigm.

Freud began the Project with an elaboration of his 1894 device of conceptualizing a quantitative factor in mental functions analogous to the flow of electric current through neuronal fibers. In the Project, he used physical analogies to conceptualize how qualitatively different mental processes located within different "spaces" of a hypothetical mental apparatus, the *mind*, were connected to changes in energy flow between hypothetical, functionally differentiated, neuronal systems. He created "a mind-robot, a thinking machine" (Erikson, 1964, p. 31) in his attempt to imagine what the unobservable mechanical dynamics of mental processes *were like*, based upon analogies to physical, spatial, energy-transfer phenomena; he was not equating the mental with the physical or reducing the mental to its physiological substrate.

For Freud, the Project was a thought experiment, a metaphorical figurative device that failed to achieve his goal of accounting for repression and defense in a mechanical model. In 1895, the year of the Project, concerning his conceptual models of the determinants of mental functions, he warned:

> All of our thinking tends to be accompanied and aided by spatial ideas … If, however, we constantly bear in mind that all such spatial relations are metaphorical and do not allow ourselves to be misled into supposing that these relations are literally present in the brain, we may nevertheless speak of a consciousness and a subconsciousness. But only on this condition. (Freud & Breuer, 1895d, p. 228)

Equally applicable to the hypothetical neuronal systems of the Project is his qualification concerning his follow-up model of a mental apparatus: "We are justified, in my view, in giving free rein to our speculations so long as we retain the coolness of our judgment and do not mistake the scaffolding for the building" (1900a, p. 536). In other words, don't take his figurative metaphorical representations literally.

In the *Naturwissenschaften* tradition of his time and culture, within his Project, Freud ambitiously attempted to create a comprehensive, integrated model of the mind as a natural machine, but it had to be a model that could accommodate his clinical theory of repression, defense, and the displacement of excessive excitation. In creating a model of the mind based on analogies to the physical world, Freud's goal was to create a conceptual framework to elucidate the hidden reality behind the appearance of consciousness, the Kantian "thing-in-itself" of unobservable, hypothetical entities and forces that determined mental functions. It was Freud's hope that his Project would provide the comprehensive natural science foundation that he believed Breuer had failed to provide for the *Studies on Hysteria*. He also hoped that it would add to the sum total of human knowledge in the field of psychology.

In his struggle to put Breuer's vague emphasis on the role of the distribution of nerve force in hysteria on an explicit, comprehensive foundation, Freud found himself caught in the dilemma of trying to reconcile explanations of mental functioning in terms of objective mechanisms and an economics of nerve force (*Naturwissenschaft*) with explanations of mental functioning in terms of personal meanings and intentions, which required subjective understanding as seen from the inside, from the point of view of the person being observed (*Geisteswissenschaft*). The search for subjective understanding was not part of *Naturwissenschaften*. Freud's clinical emphasis in *Studies on Hysteria*, his explanations of his patients' suffering in terms of their intentions and the personal meaning of their symptoms, could not be accounted for satisfactorily in an objective (from the outside) mechanical model of a hypothetical, conceptual nervous system.

Less than two months before he mailed the project to Fliess, in a moment of frustration, Freud told Fliess:

> Psychology is really a cross to bear ... All I was trying to do was to explain defense ... I had to work my way through the problem of quality, sleep, memory—in short, all of psychology. Now I want to hear no more of it. (In Masson, 1985, p. 136)

When he mailed the notebooks to Fliess he told him: "What does not yet hang together is not the mechanism—I can be patient about that—but the elucidation of repression, the clinical knowledge of which has in other respects greatly progressed" (in Masson, 1985, p. 141).

Clinically, Freud interpreted conflict, repression, and compromise formation in terms of personal meanings and intentions. If the Project's hypothetical neurons were only literal "specifiable material particles," then Freud begged the question: How did such physical entities produce human intentions or make critical judgments concerning acceptable or unacceptable meanings if their functions simply were "subject to the general laws of motion?" If the hypothetical, functionality differentiated neurons were Freud's physical metaphors for the hidden reality behind differentiated mental functions and the level of intensity of ideas, why not simply stay on psychological ground by limiting the discourse to references and terminology which applied to the psychical-mental world, the world of purpose, intention, and meaning? Freud's dilemma was his need to account for repression, in terms of intention and meaning, within the limits of a model of the mind that he believed should conform to a natural science, mechanical conception of mental functioning. For further commentary on the nature of Freud's Project see Kanzer (1973) and Geeradyn (1997).

Freud remained caught in the dilemma between mechanism and meaning throughout his career. After some continued struggle with the Project, even though he certainly maintained that brain functioning was a necessary basis for mental processes, he told Fliess in September 1898 that he "must behave as if only the psychological were under consideration" (in Masson, 1985, p. 326). In the first published presentation of his general theory of mental functioning, *The Interpretation of Dreams*, Freud stated that his attempt to understand mental functioning would stay "upon psychological ground" (p. 536). He would "avoid the temptation to determine psychical locality in any anatomical fashion" (p. 536). Instead, he used spatial-topographical and energistic (electrical and hydraulic) analogies in presenting a model of the mind as an apparatus within which different types of mental processes were located within component parts of the psyche, "the instrument which carries out our mental functions" (p. 536). In describing the functions of the psychical apparatus, Freud (1900a) offered the first published presentation of his metapsychology: a number of related hypothetical constructs that he used to conceptualize a hidden reality within the mind—mental agencies and forces (*psychic energy*) and wishes and fantasies that constitute *psychic reality*—the unknown universe behind the appearance of consciousness.

Freud's metapsychological gambit was an attempt to change the discourse of the Project from even metaphorical, neuronal terminology to strictly psychical-mental referents. Freud (1900a) now tried to explain repression "by venturing upon the hypothesis of there being two agencies," within the psychical apparatus, "one of which submitted the activity of the other to criticism which involved its exclusion from consciousness" (p. 540). However, a psychical agency which could submit another psychical agency to criticism, based on *intention* and *meaning*, and decide which meanings to exclude from consciousness (repression), was pictured by Freud as existing within a psychical apparatus based on a physiological-neural reflex model—a machine functioning to direct the discharge of energy. His metapsychological model of the mind contained an uneasy amalgam of mechanism and meaning. He could not explain his clinical insights within a mechanical mind without positioning agencies capable of intention, judgment, and censorship within the psychical apparatus, as veritable "ghosts in the machine." Freud's therapeutic methods were purely psychological, but his evolving metapsychology contained mixed physicalistic and mentalistic metaphors.

Freud developed two different kinds of theories. His metapsychology was his attempt at portraying the mind as a machine, a psychical apparatus, and his attempt to make psychoanalysis a natural science. On the other hand, his clinical theory, his theory of personal meanings, conflicts, and compromises necessary to understand the personal suffering of his patients, placed psychoanalysis in the tradition of *Geisteswissenschaften*, the human sciences. As George S. Klein (1973) pointed out: "Psychoanalysis is unique … among psychological disciplines because it contains within itself two kinds of theory, one clinical, and one metapsychological" (p. 102); a set of principles to guide clinical practice and a general theory of mental functioning. The necessity to maintain the metapsychology, and the relationship between the two theories, has been the focus of continuing debate (see Gill & Holzman, 1976). For some critiques of Freud's metapsychology see several papers by Robert Holt, found in Holt (1989, pp. 171–196, 304–344). For commentary on his confrontation with the telic (intentional) mind (see Rychlak, 1981).

In his metapsychology, Freud linked mental (psychical) processes to an organic substrate in the form of sexual physiology. He assumed the existence of some kind of mind–body interaction without an understanding of the mechanism that made interaction between the mental and the physical possible. Freud saw a pragmatic, dualistic-interactionist view, with sexual processes as the indispensable organic foundation linking mind and body as a necessary assumption for him, the medical man, to feel at ease in the life of the psyche. He saw this assumption as scientifically respectable in accordance with Du Bois-Reymond's famous 1872 pronouncement on human limits to our understanding of nature. Based upon his clinical experience, he reached his own conclusions unmoved by dogma and the opinions of proud old philosophers. And, although he did not acknowledge Brentano's influence, Aviva Cohen (2002) points out that Freud's "view of the distinction and interaction between the psychical and the physical are analogous to Brentano's teachings" (p. 92).

CHAPTER 3

Metapsychology: the interpretation of dreams

Freud had discussed the wish-fulfilling character of dreams in his unpublished Project of 1895. Early in 1898, he finished a first draft of the book, *The Interpretation of Dreams*, which would present this thesis in elaborate form. The book was completed in 1899 and published with the date, 1900. He considered this book his greatest work. Nevertheless, his claim for the complete originality of his approach to dreams is questionable. Before Freud, some of Europe's most prominent physicians anticipated him in discussing the scientific importance of dreams and dream interpretation for the exploration of the unconscious mind; for example, Charcot, Janet, and Krafft-Ebing (see Kern, 1975; Sand, 1992). Freud (1900a) did not cite them in his first chapter review of "the scientific literature on the problems of dreams." Krafft-Ebing, Freud's senior colleague at the University of Vienna, had sent him several editions of his book, *Psychopathia Sexualis*, first published in 1886. Krafft-Ebing expressed the belief that an unconscious sexual wish could be a cause of a neurotic symptom and the symptom could be a symbolic expression of the wish. Additionally, he took the position that unconscious sexual wishes could be expressed in dreams and the examination of patients' dreams provided the possibility of detecting unconscious sexual wishes that might not be discovered in any other way (see Sand, 1992).

In *The Interpretation of Dreams*, Freud presented his hierarchical, topographical (spatial) model of the mind. He assigned different mental functions and qualities to different localities within the psychical apparatus. Nevertheless, mental functioning was portrayed as a continuous, dynamic relationship between unconscious, preconscious, and conscious mental processes. Unconscious mental processes were based upon pre-linguistic, image (primary process) modes of representation. In primary process, an image was experienced with sensory qualities as though it were a real object; there is no distinction between wish and reality in the unconscious (the pleasure principle). The evolutionary, higher-level, conscious-preconscious system was based upon linguistically structured modes of representation (secondary process), where words clearly were distinguished from the objects they represented (the reality principle). Each level of mental functioning followed its own laws of association, as previously suggested by Hughlings Jackson. Freud portrayed consciousness as determined by unconscious mental processes, without concern for correlated neural substrates. See Freud (1911b) for further discussion of his two principles of mental functioning.

In presenting a spatial model of the mind, Freud (1900a) gave credit to G. T. Fechner for providing him with a starting point for conceptualizing how the qualitatively different modes of conscious thinking (secondary process), and dream thinking (primary process), could exist within the same mind. According to Freud (1900a, p. 48), Fechner (1889), in his *Psychophysik* (Vol. 2, pp. 520–521), advanced "the idea that the scene of action of dreams is different from that of waking ideational life" (p. 536). In other words, the primary process thinking experienced in dreams takes place in a different location in the mind than the location in which secondary process ideas are produced in waking life.

In the psychical apparatus, the higher-level mental agency, the conscious-preconscious system governed by linguistically structured secondary process, submitted the activity of the lower level, unconscious, primary process agency to criticism. The preconscious opposed certain unconscious wishes and directed energy, a counter-force (anticathexis), to block the force (cathexis) which would propel unacceptable wishes toward consciousness. This is the mechanism of repression. Nevertheless, certain thoughts that represented the repressed unconscious wish forced their way through in some form of compromise in dreams and in neurotic symptoms. Freud (1900a) stated: "The two psychical systems, the censorship upon the passage from one of them to the other, the inhibition and overlaying of one activity by the other ... all of these form part of the normal structure of our mental instrument" (p. 607).

During his early student days, Freud most likely was exposed to the ideas of the nineteenth-century German philosopher Herbart and his theory of unconscious mental functioning, since a textbook based upon Herbart's ideas was required reading for Freud in his last year of *Gymnasium* (high school) (Jones, 1953, p. 374). Herbart had presented a topographical, spatial model of the mind which contained many similarities to the model proposed by Freud in *The Interpretation of Dreams*. Herbart had argued that the study of mental events must include quantitative considerations. In addition, Herbart's model of the mind contained dynamic and energy-force concepts. "Mental representations which opposed each other produced conflict; 'resistance' was offered to antithetic ideas. Stronger ideas forced, or 'repressed' the weaker out of awareness or below the 'threshold' of consciousness" (Sand, 1988, p. 478; Zentner, 2002, pp. 376–378). Mental representations below the threshold of consciousness continually exerted a counter-force to propel them toward consciousness.

Ellenberger (1970) and Zentner (2002) extensively documented the popularity of the concept of unconscious mental life in the late nineteenth century, particularly among Vienna's artists and intellectuals (Kandel, 2012). Freud (1900a) singled out the philosopher Theodor Lipps for credit in this regard. He stated: "In Lipps' words ... the unconscious must be assumed to be the general basis of psychical life" (p. 612). He added: "Everything conscious has an unconscious preliminary stage; whereas what is unconscious may remain at that stage and nevertheless claim to be regarded as having a full value of a psychical process. The unconscious is the true psychical reality ..." (pp. 612–613). The unconscious is the Kantian, unknown, "thing in itself," behind the appearance of consciousness; "*in its innermost nature it is as much unknown to us as the reality of the external world, and it is as incompletely presented by the data of consciousness as is the external world by the communications of our sense organs*" (p. 613, Freud's italics).

Freud (1900a) argued that the "core of our being" in the uncon-scious is wishful impulses derived from the earliest years of our lives (pp. 603–604). Sexual wishes from childhood have been subjected to repression because their fulfillment is unacceptable to the secondary process, preconscious-conscious system. Nevertheless, these wishful impulses "can neither be destroyed nor inhibited" (p. 604), and in spite of the counter-force produced by the preconscious to exclude them from consciousness, substitute thoughts, which, by association, became "the vehicles of the unconscious wish, force their way through in some form of compromise," as may be seen in neurotic symptoms (p. 605). Fur-thermore, he stressed that his theory of the psychoneuroses asserted that it was

> an indisputable and invariable fact that only sexual wishful impulses from infancy, which have undergone repression ... dur-ing the developmental period of childhood, are capable of being revived during *later* developmental periods ... and are thus able to furnish the motive force for the formation of psychoneurotic symptoms of every kind. (pp. 605–606)

In this view, traumatic memories were no longer the prerequisite for adult defense neurosis. Rather, defenses against unacceptable childhood sexual wishes and fantasies (possibly related to childhood autoerotic activity) were the precipitator of adult psychoneurotic symptoms. While he argued that dream wishes invariably derived from the unconscious, at this point he left open the question of the extent to which it was child-hood sexual wishes that were the basis for dreams.

In presenting his view that dreams were disguised fulfillments of unconscious wishes, Freud distinguished between the remembered dream, the manifest content, and the hidden wishes symbolically rep-resented in the manifest content, the latent content. The preconscious censorship system masked unconscious primary process wishes by allowing only visual images that were unrecognized symbolic represen-tations of the unconscious wish to appear in the dream. Dream symbols, primary process images perceived as real objects, were formed through the *dream work* which consisted in the process of pictorial representa-tion, condensation, and displacement. Through condensation a number of unconscious ideas were compressed into one visual symbol through which they all were represented simultaneously. Through displacement, attention in the dream was redirected (misdirected) away from symbols close to the unconscious wish to more remotely associated images, and emotions were redirected from significant images toward less significant images, hiding real emotional connections and meanings which were unacceptable to the preconscious censorship system. Now, the psychical apparatus that carried out the dream work "began to sound more like a poet than a machine" (Phillips, 2014, p. 110).

For example, Freud (1900a) reported a dream told to him by a young woman who was not neurotic but was of a prudish and reserved character. She was engaged to be married, but there were difficulties that were likely to lead to a postponement of the marriage. She reported the dream: "*I arrange the centre of a table with flowers for a birthday*" (p. 374). According to Freud, the dream was an expression of her bridal wishes: "the table with its floral centre-piece symbolized herself and her genitals; she represented her wishes for the future as fulfilled, for her thoughts were already occupied with the birth of a baby; so her marriage lay a long way behind her" (p. 374). The woman reported that the flowers included "lilies of the valley" and "violets." Freud interpreted the symbolism of the flowers as representing the woman's virginity and defloration—the lilies of the valley represented the purity of her virginity and the violets the violence of defloration. The arranging for a birthday in the dream meant that the woman was identifying herself with her fiancé, "was representing him as 'arranging' her for a birth—that is, as copulating with her" (p. 376). The dream gave expression to thoughts of sexual love that Freud believed the woman was too inhibited to think about in her waking life; the dream expressed her wishes for copulation and her fear of being deflowered.

Freud's approach to the interpretation of dreams was based upon his assumption that strict determinism holds sway in the mind; there were no chance mental events. The manifest content of a dream always was determined by unconscious wishes and the unconscious mechanisms of the dream work. He believed that by interpreting the meaning of dream symbols and associated patterns of free associations, he could infer hidden wishes, conflicts, and meanings behind the seemingly irrational manifest content of dreams.

A year after the publication of *The Interpretation of Dreams*, Freud extended his theory of the unconscious determination of mental events when he published his book, *The Psychopathology of Everyday Life*. Here he argued that normal, everyday, seemingly irrational mental events, such as slips of the tongue, were representations of unconscious wishes and inner conflicts. Freud (1901b) stated: "If we give way to the view that a part of our psychical functioning cannot be explained by purposive ideas, we are failing to appreciate the extent of determination in mental life" (p. 240). For example, when a speaker consciously intended to say one thing but instead said another, the slip of the tongue was an unconsciously intentionally determined expression of an unconscious wish, a "Freudian slip." When a master of ceremonies introduced Mr. Jones by exclaiming: "Ladies and gentlemen, I would like to *prevent* Mr. Jones," instead of the consciously intended *present* Mr. Jones, the slip of the tongue was not an innocent error, it was an indication of the master of ceremonies' unconscious wish concerning Mr. Jones.

In addition to slips of the tongue, in *The Psychopathology of Everyday Life*, Freud (1901b) also discussed the forgetting of names, misreadings and slips of the pen, and a variety of bungled or faulty actions. In each of these situations, he attempted to apply his new paradigm, which was to demonstrate how unconscious wishes and psychodynamic processes could interfere with everyday normal psychical functions and produce malfunctions of memory, the substitution of one word for another in reading, writing, or speaking, and faulty actions such as losing someone's address or getting on the wrong train on the way home. In all such cases, Freud argued, an unconscious wish was being expressed in a disguised manner, as was the case in dreams and psychoneurotic symptoms (see also Freud, 1916–17, pp. 15–79).

In *Jokes and Their Relation to the Unconscious*, Freud (1905c) applied his conception of the unconscious determination of mental events to an analysis of humor. As was the case with dreams, he argued that jokes were compromise formations which provided an indirect way to express symbolically unacceptable sexual or aggressive wishes that could not be expressed directly without provoking anxiety or punishment. For example, a sexual wish might be expressed indirectly through the joke: "She has boyfriends by the score, and most of them do." Aggressive impulses might be expressed by such jokes as: "I take my wife out every night, but she always finds her way home," or "My husband is a model husband, just not a working model." For commentary on Freud's theory of humor and his frequent use of jokes, see Oring (1984).

Over the years Freud modified his view on the wish-fulfilling function of dreams. In paragraphs he added to *The Interpretation of Dreams* in 1919, he offered his view that unpleasurable dreams might be "punishment dreams." "What is fulfilled in them is equally an unconscious wish, namely a wish that the dreamer may be punished for a repressed and forbidden wishful impulse" (1900a, p. 557). With the development of structural theory in 1923, to be discussed below, Freud postulated the existence of an unconscious anti-libidinal force which he called the superego that opposed the expression of repressed forbidden wishes. With structural theory, punishment dreams could be seen as an effort to satisfy the demands of the superego in order to preserve parental love and avoid guilt.

In *Beyond the Pleasure Principle*, Freud (1920g) confronted traumatic dreams in which the dreamer experienced painful scenes from the past. Such dreams occurred in traumatic neuroses, for example, among war veterans reliving combat experiences, or among patients undergoing psychoanalysis who confronted childhood traumas. Freud stated: "This would seem to be the place, then, at which to admit for the first time an exception to the proposition that dreams are fulfillments of wishes" (p. 32). "We may assume," he reported, "that dreams are here helping to carry out another task ... These dreams are endeavouring to master the stimulus retrospectively ..." (p. 32). In other words, the function of traumatic dreams was to master trauma rather than to obtain gratification of wishes for pleasure or punishment.

With his invocation of structural theory in 1923, Freud distinguished between dreams *from above* and dreams *from below*. Dreams which arise from below are "provoked by the strength of an unconscious (repressed) wish" (Freud, 1923b, p. 111). In structural theory, dreams from below arise from the id (to be discussed below). Dreams from above arise from the ego as attempts to deal with recent experiences, to achieve mastery over traumatic experiences, and to appease the moral demands of the superego. See McLeod (1992) for a review of the evolution of Freud's theory of dreams.

In the essay "The Unconscious," Freud (1915e) expanded on the topographic point of view first published in 1900 in *The Interpretation of Dreams.* "The nucleus of the Ucs. consists of instinctual representatives which seek to discharge their cathexis; that is to say, it consists of wishful impulses" (p. 186). He also described the different qualities attributed to psychic functioning according to whether the functioning was truly unconscious or merely preconscious (pp. 186–189). What was truly unconscious, or dynamically unconscious, was primary process wishful images experienced as reality: *psychic reality*, the hidden domain of fantasy and dream work. What was merely preconscious, or only descriptively unconscious, was secondary process, linguistically structured thought that was in the form required to make access to consciousness a possibility, if not necessarily a certainty.

CHAPTER 4

Motivation and conflict: the instinctual drives

I n *Three Essays on the Theory of Sexuality*, Freud remained consistent in his pragmatic, mind–body, dualist-interactionist viewpoint when he introduced his concept of the sexual instinctual drive, a motivational force in mental activity. He explained (1905d):

> By an "instinct" is provisionally to be understood the psychical representative of an endosomatic, continuously flowing source of stimulation ... the concept of the instinct is thus one of those lying on the frontier between the mental and the physical ... The source of an instinct is a process of excitation occurring in an organ and the immediate aim of the instinct lies in the removal of this organic stimulus. (p. 168)

The unconscious mind where the sexual instinctual drive was expressed was seen to be full of wishful images, representing sexual, need-satisfying objects required for actions which discharged sexual energy. The expression of the sexual drive had to be controlled and directed by the evolutionary higher level preconscious-conscious system.

In his metapsychological paper, "Instincts and Their Vicissitudes," Freud (1915c) further explained that

> an 'instinct' appears to us as a concept on the frontier between the mental and the somatic, as the psychical representative of the stimuli originating from within the organism and reaching the mind, as a measure of the demand made upon the mind for work in consequence of its connection with the body. (pp. 121–122)

An instinct has an *aim*, an *object*, and a *source*. The instinctual *aim* is the removal of tension subjectively experienced within the body. The *object* is the means by which tension reduction can be achieved, that is, by directing actions toward objects in the external world, or toward one's own body. The *source* is the somatic process which generated the energy (excitation) responsible for the subjectively experienced inner tension. While the source and aim of an instinct remained constant, the energy generated by the source of the instinct can be discharged in a variety of ways because many different objects and activities can be substituted for the original object and activity which first was associated with the removal of the particular tension. He (1915e) insisted that: "An instinct can never become an object of consciousness—only the idea that represents the instinct can. Even in the unconscious, moreover, an instinct cannot be represented otherwise than by an idea" (p. 177).

Because, for Freud, many different objects and activities can be substituted for the original sexual, instinctual need satisfying objects and activities, Jonathan Lear (2005) has pointed out, in Freud's view:

> Human sexuality in its very nature is open to variation. Overall, what is getting selected is an inextricable entanglement of sexuality and imagination. Unlike other animals, human sexuality is essentially imaginative—that is, it is essentially open to imaginative variability. One consequence is that all sorts of activities are going to count as sexual that have no relation to reproduction. (p. 78)

As stated above, in tracing mental life to a somatic ground, Freud theorized that the deep interior of the unconscious mind contained wishful images which were demands upon mental life that originated in the interior of the body. Even though he viewed demands for tension reduction as emanating from the physical side, starting with physiological changes in the material body, his psychological-level approach anchored the unconscious mind to the interior of the body defined as a person's *subjective experience of one's body as lived from within* (Draenos, 1982). Freud's pragmatic, dualist-interactionist approach maintained a distinction between the material body and the mental-subjective world which included the subjective experience of the inside of one's body. Freud's psychological approach to the instinctual drive as the somatic demand upon mental life focused on what went on *within the mind*, the activation of object-intentional thought—wishes and desires for objects and activities necessary to reduce tensions experienced within the lived-in body, caused by physiological changes in the material body. Whereas in writing about hysteria, he focused on the effect of the mind upon the body; in conceptualizing the sexual instinctual drive, Freud focused on the influence of changes in the body upon activity within the mind (Silverstein, 1985, 2003; Elisha, 2011; Sugarman, 2016). As characterized by Marcia Cavell (1993): "Instinct is Freud's weasel word, the courier for negotiating the dark passage between body and mind" (p. 55).

Sándor Ferenczi, a close collaborator and confidant of Freud for over twenty-five years, offered the following account of how Freud's instinctual drive concept served him in conceptualizing a connection between mind and body. Ferenczi (1933) stated, "Dislike of unfounded generalization guarded Freud from the error of uniting prematurely the mental and physical into materialistic monism, as was customary in other quarters." He recognized:

the fact that mental life was accessible only through introspective methods, that is, from the subjective side; further, that facts that become accessible through subjective methods must be fully accepted as psychic reality. Thus, Freud became a dualist, a term which most physical scientists have regarded, and still regard, as almost opprobrious. I do not believe that Freud objected essentially to the monistic conception of knowledge. His dualism says only that unification is not possible at present, nor in the near future, and perhaps cannot be ever achieved completely. On no account should we confuse Freud's dualism with the naïve separation of a living organism into a body and a mind. He is always

mindful of the anatomic-physiological facts concerning the nervous system. He pursues his psychological investigations up to
the point of human impulses, which he looks upon as a dividing
line between the mental and the physical, a line which he does
not believe psychological interpretation should cross, because
as yet it seems incompetent to do so. On the other hand, just as
his metapsychological system, which is constructed on the pattern of the reflex arc, shows, he must rely on analogies to natural
science even in his purely psychological investigations. (p. 147;
see Silverstein, 1997)

In a similar vein, Alfred Tauber (2010) observed:

Basically, Freud divided the mind between the unconscious
grounded in the biological and thus subject to some natural causation, and a rational faculty which lodges itself in consciousness
and exists independent of natural cause. The critical distinction
resides in Freud's acceptance, as a *psychologist*, of a functional
mind–body dualism, and in the higher functions of the mind,
he places the repository of interpretative reason. (p. 116, italics
in original)

Freud (1910i) expanded his theory of human motivation by proposing a
dualistic division of instinctual drives into two categories: *ego instincts*,
in the service of the preservation of the individual's life; and *sexual
instincts*, directed toward the attainment of pleasure (and species preservation). The striving for pleasure and tension reduction underwent
developmental transformations correlated with the maturation of the
child's erogenous zones. He used the term "libido" to refer to the energy
(force) of the sexual instinct.

Freud bridged the gap between mind and body with his concept
of instinctual drives (*Triebe*), and also used his dualistic drive concept
to explain why, in his view, it was human nature to be in conflict with
society and, through socialization, to be in conflict with oneself. Ego
instincts inevitably came into conflict with sexual instincts: the need for
self-preservation—the avoidance of punishment and guilt—required

repression of forbidden and taboo thoughts that directed us toward childhood sexual objects and the pursuit of sexual pleasure through the stimulation of pregenital erogenous zones. The dynamic power of unsuccessfully repressed childhood sexual wishes was the force behind neurotic symptoms.

Freud twice revised his dualistic conception of basic human motivation. In "On Narcissism" (1914c), he introduced a new division of instinctual drives: *ego, libido* (self-love, self-preservation) versus *object libido* (other love, species preservation).

Because Freud had written "On Narcissism" (1914c) more because of the pressure of rival theorists' ideas than because of the pressure of facts, his zealous defense of sexual libido resulted in a weakening of his previous dualistic instinctual drive theory that had postulated a clear distinction between a driving force which was sexual and a restraining force which was not sexual, with qualitatively different energies at the roots of sexual and ego drives. Now it appeared there was only one group of drives all energized by libido. His conception of psychic conflict, defense, and compromise still required a mental structure that was attuned to reality and that could oppose the sexual drive by means of its own source of energy. In 1914, Freud wrote to a colleague: "Your acceptance of my 'Narcissism' affected me deeply ... I have a strong feeling of its serious inadequacy" (in Abraham & E. L. Freud, 1965, pp. 170–171). A recognition of the theoretical fuzziness that he had created in 1914 required him to embark on later revisions in his conception of the instinctual drives, and in 1923 he developed structural theory which will be discussed below.

In *Beyond the Pleasure Principle*, Freud (1920g) introduced the final revision of his concept of basic human motivation. Here he introduced a new dualism of instinctual drives, a progressive Eros, the *life instinct* (including ego libido versus object libido); a binding force that reaches out to the world to create unities, versus an entropic, regressive, unity-destroying Thanatos (with cosmic overtones), the *death instinct* (including self-directed versus other-directed aggression). Now, he tried to restore a dualistic opposition between a force that was sexual, the *life instinct*, opposed by a force that was not sexual, the *death instinct*. If the life instinct remained strong, some of the force of the death instinct would be deflected away from the self toward others. The deflected force of the death instinct was a powerful source of aggressive behavior that could become violent and destructive (see Brown, 1959, pp. 77–86).

The death instinct concept gave him a new basis for explaining the existence of a regressive force in human nature, *the repetition compulsion*, a compulsion to repeat behavior patterns related to unresolved conflicts (fixations) from pregenital stages of development, and a basis for revisiting earlier traumas in dreams. Whereas Jung had argued that neurotic adults only retrospectively sexualized memories of childhood, Freud responded by asserting that neurotic adults were caught in a regressive repetition compulsion to express actual sexual and aggressive impulses from childhood which they had not brought under proper control, and which now they expressed symbolically through their compromise formation symptoms. In addition, by making the death instinct a source of aggression, Freud was responding to a challenge from Alfred Adler who downplayed sexuality and made an aggressive drive a primary force in human motivation (see Stepansky, 1977, 1983).

Besides responding to the challenge from Adler, the unprecedented slaughter and carnage of World War I (1914–1918), during a purported age of enlightenment, had to influence Freud to conceive that his proposed death instinct, with its outwardly directed aggression, was rooted in human nature. The dangers and privations his family experienced, caused by the war, affected him deeply. His sons were serving in the Austrian army. In January 1919, he dejectedly wrote to Ernest Jones:

> These last months are becoming the worst we have had to endure while this war lasted. My eldest son is still a prisoner in Italy. We are all of us slowly failing in health and bulk, not alone so in this town I assure you. Prospects are dark. (In Jones, 1955, p. 205)

Prospects were dark for Freud. In 1923 he was diagnosed with squamous cell carcinoma, cancer of the palate. He underwent repeated surgical procedures and suffered continuing pain and discomfort for sixteen years. In spite of his condition, he continued to write, revise, and expand the scope of his theories until his death in 1939.

CHAPTER 5

The riddle of hypnosis

Freud's thinking about mind–body issues in hypnosis evolved with his theorizing concerning childhood sexuality and human evolution (Silverstein & Silverstein, 1990). In his paper "Psychical (or Mental) Treatment" (1890a), he noted that, in the hypnotic state: "the influence of the mind over the body is extraordinarily increased" (p. 295). This demonstrated "an increase in the physical influence of an idea" (p. 296).

As to why a hypnotist could exert power over a subject to accept his suggested *ideas*, as if they were his own, Freud observed

> credulity such as the subject has in relation to his hypnotist is shown only by a child towards his beloved parents, and that an attitude of similar subjection on the part of one person towards another has only one parallel, though a complete one—namely in certain love relationships where there is extreme devotion. (p. 296)

By 1905, in *Three Essays on the Theory of Sexuality*, with his proposal that children experienced sexual desire for the parent, Freud offered an explanation for the "credulous submissiveness shown by a hypnotized subject towards his hypnotist ... the essence of hypnosis lies in an unconscious fixation of the subject's libido to the figure of the hypnotist" (p. 150). In this explanation, a hypnotized subject accepts suggestions from the hypnotist as if he were a loved parent. The subject transferred sexual desire for the parent toward the hypnotist and behaved in a compliant manner so as to win that person's love.

In *Group Psychology and the Analysis of the Ego* (1921c), Freud invoked his theoretical view of human evolution (see Silverstein, 1989b, 2003) to further explain the power of hypnosis. He asserted that the submissive posture adopted by a hypnotized subject was not only a reenactment of a child's attitude toward its parents, but also the activation of a universally inherited predisposition to reenact a submissive stance toward the "primal father." Previously, in *Totem and Taboo* (1912–13), he had proposed that the original social organization of the human species was the primal horde, groups ruthlessly dominated by one male, the "primal father." He further reasoned that modern humans inherited characteristics that their ancestors acquired by behaving in a certain manner during the early prehistory of the species. Thus, he saw humans as born with a predisposition to reenact a submissive stance toward the "primal father" and, therefore, become subject to accepting direct suggestions from a hypnotist. The hypnotist became, in effect, the "primal father."

CHAPTER 6

Structural theory

In 1923, in the *Ego and the Id*, Freud created his final model of the mind, the structural model. He supplemented his topographic model which represented mental functioning with the spatial metaphor of levels—unconscious, preconscious, and conscious—with a hypothetical set of interactive agencies: the *id* (the "it"), the *ego* (the "I"), and the *superego* (the "above I"). Topographically, the id was pictured at the bottom and was characterized by the evolutionary lower-level mental functions he previously had attributed to the unconscious. The id was the locus of wishful image object representations correlated with the satisfaction of bodily needs, generated by underlying physiological processes. The id functioned unconsciously, following the pleasure principle—the wishful image was experienced as the real object (primary process).

Topographically, the ego was pictured as developing essentially above the id; however, the ego functioned at all topographical levels, that is, a portion of the ego immediately above the id functioned unconsciously, while above the unconscious ego there were portions of the ego functioning at the preconscious and conscious levels. The evolutionary higher-level ego utilized linguistically structured thought patterns (secondary process), and it followed the reality principle. The task of the ego was to match the images (wishes) of the id with appropriate objects in the real world, and to obtain satisfaction of bodily needs with minimum cost in terms of punishment or guilt through successful compromise formation. The superego, functioning unconsciously, consisted of moralistic demands: moral dos (an ego ideal), and moral don'ts (a conscience), internalized through identification with a parent.

Freud created the hypothetical agencies of the ego and the id to reconcile a contradiction in his topographical model. As we have seen, he had written of the conscious-preconscious system as repressing the unconscious. However, the logic of his position required that both the *repressing process* and *repressed content* had to be truly *unconscious*, but they had to be separated and differentiated. He now assigned the function of repression to the ego, to that part of the ego which operated unconsciously but was still subject to secondary process rules. The content which was repressed was assigned to the lower-level unconscious id which functioned according to primary process rules. Because the ego functioned partly unconsciously, partly preconsciously, and only partly consciously, the unconscious ego, unknown to consciousness, controlled access to the preconscious level, the gateway to consciousness. Thus, consciousness was shaped by unknown, unconscious ego functions.

According to Freud (1923b):

> We have come upon something in the ego itself which is also unconscious, which behaves exactly like the repressed—that is, which produces powerful effects without itself being conscious and which requires special work before it can be made conscious … we land in endless obscurities and difficulties if we keep to our habitual forms of expression and try, for instance, to derive neuroses from a conflict between the conscious and the unconscious. We shall have to substitute for this antithesis another … the antithesis between the coherent ego and the repressed which is split off from it. (p. 17)

Earlier, by 1919, when he was writing *Beyond the Pleasure Principle* (1920g), Freud already realized that it had become necessary to "correct a shortcoming in our terminology. We shall avoid a lack of clarity if we make our contrast not between the conscious and the unconscious but between the coherent ego and the repressed" (p. 19).

Now that he had distinguished between the ego and the id, Freud (1923b) tried to resolve questions dating back to "On Narcissism" (1914c) concerning the source of energy for each of his newly hypothesized agencies.

> At the very beginning, all the libido is accumulated in the id, while the ego is still in the process of formation or is still feeble. The id sends part of this libido out into erotic object-cathexis, whereupon the ego, now grown stronger, tries to get hold of this object-libido and to force itself on the id as a love-object. (1923b, p. 46)

The ego therefore derives its energy from the id, but the ego can use this derived energy to try to control the id, even to oppose the id in the service of self-preservation.

> By thus getting hold of the libido from the object-cathexis, setting itself up as sole love-object, and desexualizing or sublimating the libido of the id, the ego is working in opposition to the purposes of Eros and placing itself at the service of the opposing instinctual impulses. (p. 46)

Nevertheless, the ego must serve the id; it must use its desexualized libido to find appropriate satisfactions for the needs of the body which initially are represented psychically, symbolically as primary process within the id; "the ego, by sublimating some of the libido for its self and its purposes, assists the id in its work of mastering the tensions" (p. 47).

Freud's continued reliance on energy-force concepts in his metapsychology and his continued viewing of the mind as an energy-driven machine which had to direct the discharge of energy to relieve bodily tensions, forced him to wrestle with questions concerning the nature and sources of energy for his hypothetical mental structures or agencies. He continued to make pronouncements on these issues which sometimes appeared to be conflicting views (see Freud, 1923b, pp. 63–66), but the statements in the paragraph above seem to be his most consistent position on the energy sources for the ego and the id.

In proposing the superego which functioned unconsciously but was not repressed nor part of the repressing ego, Freud responded to a challenge from C. G. Jung concerning the existence of archaic, archetypal, universally inherited, transpersonal structures in the unconscious. He also was responding to Jung's denial of the actual sexual nature of the childhood Oedipus complex. He argued that the superego was the legacy of the childhood Oedipus complex, which actually was sexual, and which all humans were predisposed to experience personally through the transpersonal inheritance of acquired characteristics (Silverstein, 1986, 1989b, 2003). The Oedipus complex was properly resolved through repression, sublimation, and identification with the same-sexed parent. For Freud, the archetypal element in the development of the superego was the predisposition to repeat in one's individual development (ontogeny) events which the human species acted out as the species developed (phylogeny) (see Silverstein, 1986, 1989b, 2003).

Freud argued that not only were humans born with predispositions to experience incestuous and parricidal impulses that reflected behavior which actually was carried out in early human primal hordes; they also were born with the predisposition to internalize taboos against such behaviors that also were developed by our early human ancestors. But, he insisted, the internalization of such taboos was not simply the direct actualization of a phylogenetic inheritance; the internalization of taboos against incest and parricide required that, as children, individuals actually experienced forbidden sexual and aggressive impulses directed toward their parents: the Oedipus complex. Children had to properly repress and sublimate these sexual impulses and, through identification with the same-sexed parent, redirect aggression away from parents toward one's self. This redirection of aggression led to the formation of the unconscious moralistic superego, the autonomous offspring of the self-observing ego. The superego directed previously parentally targeted aggression toward one's own ego, in opposition to the expression of forbidden sexual and aggressive impulses. Critical opposition from the superego caused the ego to experience a form of anxiety called guilt. Failure to resolve the Oedipus complex properly created a predisposition toward adult psychoneuroses.

In a footnote added in 1920 to *Three Essays on the Theory of Sexuality*, as part of his combat with Alfred Adler and Jung, Freud (1905d) stressed the point that the Oedipus complex represents

> the peak of infantile sexuality, which, through its after-effects, exercises a decisive influence on the sexuality of adults … the importance of the Oedipus complex has become more and more clearly evident; its recognition has become the shibboleth that distinguishes the adherents of psycho-analysis from its opponents. (p. 226n.)

In 1926, in *Inhibitions, Symptoms and Anxiety*, Freud proposed the last major revision in his metapsychology. Previously, he had conceptualized anxiety as transformed undischarged sexual excitation. With his new structural model, he now was required to make the ego the seat of anxiety. He now conceptualized anxiety as a danger signal experienced by the ego. The ego could experience anxiety in relation to three types of danger: real external threat, the possibility of the failure of repression, or moral objections from the superego. The primary task of the ego was seen as mediating between the conflicting demands of reality, the id, and the superego, and minimizing the experience of anxiety. The ego functioned to minimize the experience of anxiety by maximizing instinctual gratification, with the minimum cost in terms of punishment and guilt.

With structural theory, the ego controlled consciousness: if the ego did not translate a pictorial primary process thought which had sensory qualities into a secondary process linguistic form, that thought was denied access to consciousness. It was unknown, unconscious ego-functioning which made repression, compromise, and defense possible. Psychoneurotic symptoms were defenses against anxiety, arising from an internal conflict among the ego, the id, and the superego. Psychoneurotic symptoms were symbolic expressions of a psychical conflict between impulses in the id that originated in childhood and the controlling ego. Psychoneurotic symptoms were compromises between wish and defense.

Concerning psychoneuroses (defense neuroses), Freud (1926d) now believed that: "It was anxiety which produced repression and not, as I formerly believed, repression which produced anxiety" (pp. 108–109).

Here, Freud appeared to give up his long-held belief that anxiety was transformed libido which was blocked by repression, since it was anxiety as a danger signal in the ego which caused repression in the first place.

In *New Introductory Lectures on Psycho-Analysis*, when considering the relationship between repression and anxiety, Freud (1933a) reminded the reader of his earlier hypothesis that it was the libidinal charge (the energy) connected with the instinctual impulse that was being fought against that was transformed by repression into anxiety. "We no longer feel able to say that" (p. 91). Now, a distinction had to be made between original repressions and later repressions. In later repression "anxiety is awakened as a signal of an earlier situation of danger. The first and original (primal) repressions arise directly from traumatic moments, when the ego meets with an excessively great libidinal demand" (p. 94). Later repressions construct this anxiety anew as a warning of a new upsurge of this excessively great libidinal demand.

Freud (1933a) summarized his new position on anxiety by stating that he now conceptualized "a twofold origin of anxiety—one as a direct consequence of the traumatic moment and the other as a signal threatening a repetition of such a moment" (pp. 94–95). Now, he viewed anxiety as a warning signal within the ego over potential loss of control over drive-derivative sexual impulses (the return of the repressed); over demands from the superego; and over the anticipation of other internal or external sources of tension or pain.

CHAPTER 7

The defensive ego

After Freud revised his theory of anxiety in *Inhibitions, Symptoms and Anxiety* (1926d), the main concern of Freudian theory shifted from a focus on the instinctual drives to a focus on the functions of the mental structures, the id, the ego, the superego, and their relations with each other. The major concern became the functions of the ego in controlling the instinctual drives and forming compromises acceptable within the moral restrictions imposed by the superego.

Ideally, the adult ego should respond to anxiety, the warning signals of danger, by adopting problem-solving methods that are congruent with reality. If the ego is overwhelmed by anxiety because of its weakness in confronting dangers from the external world, the power of unconscious instinctual impulses, or moral demands from the superego, the ego may attempt to reduce anxiety by employing tactics that deny or distort reality. The reality-denying or -distorting methods used by the ego to reduce anxiety were named the defense mechanisms of the ego.

Since 1895, the time of writing *Studies on Hysteria*, the concept of the defense mechanism of repression had been the foundation stone of Freud's clinical theory. In his metapsychological paper, "Repression" (1915d), he distinguished between primal repression and repression proper. Primal repression was the normally expected repression of sexual wishes in early childhood necessary to resolve the Oedipus complex. He stated (1915d): "We have reason to assume that there is a *primal repression*, a first phase of repression, which consists in the psychical (ideational) representative of the instinct being denied entrance into the conscious" (p. 148). Later repressions or "*repression proper*, affects mental derivatives of the repressed representative, or such trains of thought as, originating elsewhere, have come into associative connection with it … Repression proper, therefore, is actually an after-pressure" (p. 148).

In *Inhibitions, Symptoms and Anxiety*, Freud (1926d) elaborated on the role of repression proper or secondary repression, in causing neurosis: "most of the repressions with which we have to deal in our therapeutic work are cases of *after*-pressure. They presuppose the operation of earlier, *primal repressions* … A symptom arises from an instinctual impulse which has been detrimentally affected by repression" (p. 94). When primal repression is successful because instinctual impulses have been sublimated, neurosis is avoided. However, in those cases in which the ego has lost control over repressed impulses, "in which repression must be described as having to a greater or less extent failed …" neurotic symptoms appear because, in this event "the instinctual impulse has found a substitute in spite of repression …" (p. 95). The unsuccessfully repressed instinctual impulse, over which the ego has lost influence, connects itself to other psychical processes producing psychical derivatives that take its place. These psychical derivatives may break through "into the ego and into consciousness in the form of an unrecognizably distorted substitute …" creating a psychoneurotic symptom (Freud, 1926e, p. 203).

Primal repression and the sublimation of the repressed instinctual impulses, that is, the substituting of socially approved object-choices and behaviors for unacceptable unconscious wishes and impulses, were considered by Freud to be necessary ego defenses and, when accomplished successfully, the basis for mental health. In primal repression, early primary process wishes that produced anxiety in the ego were never translated into secondary process forms, so they never achieved consciousness. That is why, according to Freud, an adult cannot remember the pregenital wishes of childhood that were subjected to primal repression.

All ego defense mechanisms were compromises between driving and restraining forces. All ego defense mechanisms involved some degree of self-deception concerning one's true wishes and feelings. Since healthy psychosexual development required primal repression and sublimation of oedipal and other pregenital wishes and impulses, Freud saw the self-deception inherent in these ego defenses as a prerequisite for normal development. What distinguished the healthy person from the neurotic individual was the degree of self-deception that resulted from the ego defenses employed in response to the pressure of instinctual drives. The healthy individual had established successful primal repressions and sublimations in early childhood. Hysterical patients, on the other hand, fell back on repression proper (secondary repression) in dealing with anxiety over derivatives of instinctual drives, and they represented repressed instinctual impulses symbolically through conversion into compromise formation physical symptoms. Freud's therapeutic goal was to reduce an individual's self-deception by strengthening the ego to better cope with unconscious forces; to liberate the person to put into words true feelings and desires and to work them through within the analytic relationship; to stop living in the present *as if it were the past*.

CHAPTER 8

Civilization and Dr. Freud's discontents

reud left us with a tragic view of human nature; in other words, to be human is to be in conflict with society and within oneself. Society necessarily opposes the uncontrolled expression of the instinctual drives of the individual for the common good; however, the instinctual drives are selfish in that they press for immediate satisfaction to lower the levels of tension within the individual. The implication of this inevitable state of conflict, according to Freud, is that certain forms of compromise between desire (wish) and defense (sublimations) are the necessary basis for ordinary happiness and the avoidance of neurotic misery. For Freud, the happiness that is possible, is defined as *the avoidance of neurotic misery*. In *Civilization and Its Discontents* (1930a), he offered his view that:

> The programme of becoming happy which the pleasure principle imposes on us, cannot be fulfilled; yet we must not—indeed, we cannot—give up our efforts to bring it nearer to fulfilment by some means or other. Very different paths may be taken in that direction, and we may give priority either to the positive aspect of the aim, that of gaining pleasure, or to its negative one, that of avoiding

unpleasure. By none of these paths can we obtain all that we desire. Happiness, in the reduced sense in which we recognize it as possible, is a problem of the economics of the individual's libido. (p. 83)

For Freud, that's life. That's the way it is. For him, that's the way it was.

Freud freely confessed his feelings of sexual frustration and discontent with his marriage in his letters to Wilhelm Fliess. After the birth of five children in rapid succession, because he was very resistant to using available means of birth control (see McLaren, 1979), in August, 1893 he admitted that, to prevent more pregnancies, he and his wife were "now living in abstinence" (in Masson, 1985, p. 54). In October, 1897 at age forty-one, he confided: "Sexual excitement ... is no longer of use for someone like me" (in Masson, 1985, p. 276). In March, 1900 he told Fliess: "You know how limited my pleasures are ... I am done begetting children ..." (in Masson, 1985, p. 404). By 1908, in what might be considered autobiographical, Freud wrote:

> satisfying sexual intercourse in marriage takes place only for a few years and we must subtract from this, of course, the intervals of abstention necessitated by regard for the wife's health. After these three, four or five years, the marriage becomes a failure in so far as it has promised the satisfaction of sexual needs. For all the devices hitherto invented for preventing conception impair sexual enjoyment, hurt the fine susceptibilities of both partners and eventually cause illness. (p. 194)

As early as the 1890s, Freud had concluded that enforced sexual abstinence in marriage produced "anxiety neurosis," and coitus interruptus to prevent pregnancy was also likely to produce "anxiety neurosis." He believed, for men, "This is often corrected, as it were, by normal coitus outside marriage" (Freud, 1893, in Masson, 1985, p. 183).

In 1905, Freud submitted written replies to questions on sexual morality posed by a Vienna commission of inquiry concerning possible changes in the marriage laws: his answers were made public on February 8, 1905 (see Freud's statements in Boyer, 1978, pp. 91–93). He argued that demands for involuntary sexual abstinence were damaging, leading to "a disposition to various forms of nervousness" (p. 93).

In addition, "The existence of a marriage is in itself no grounds for sexual obligations when the marriage no longer fulfills the task of satisfying normal sexual instincts" (p. 93).

Considering Freud's sexual frustration in his marriage, and his justifications for sex outside marriage when the marriage no longer fulfilled a man's sexual needs, it is not unreasonable to believe that he may have sought sexual satisfaction in an affair with his sister-in-law Minna Bernays (see Swales, 1982a, 2003). She lived in his home from 1896. Starting in 1898 they occasionally traveled abroad alone together as a couple. Perhaps Freud had Minna in mind when he wrote:

> It sounds not only disagreeable but also paradoxical, yet it must nevertheless be said that anyone who is to be really free and happy in love must have surmounted his respect for women and have come to terms with the idea of incest with his mother or sister. (1912d, p. 186)

He also may have had Minna in mind when in 1915 he wrote to James Jackson Putnam, "I stand for a much freer sexual life. However, I have made little use of such freedom, except insofar as I was convinced of what was *permissible for me* in this area" (in Hale, 1971, p. 189). Accusations and evidence for a long-rumored sexual relationship between Freud and Minna are reviewed in Silverstein (2007). See also Gale (2016) and Billig (2019, pp. 79–112).

If the demands of Eros did not create enough conflict, Freud (1930a) warned us about the dangers from our other side, the power of Thanatos, the death instinct.

> The fateful question for the human species seems to me to be whether and to what extent their cultural development will succeed in mastering the disturbance of their communal life by the instinct of aggression and self-destruction … Men have gained control over the forces of nature to such an extent that with their help they would have no difficulty in exterminating one another to the last man. They know this, and hence comes a large part of their current unrest, their unhappiness and their mood of anxiety. (p. 145)

Part II

Freud on sexuality and neuroses

Introduction

In Part I we followed Freud's development of his metapsychology—his psychology of unconscious mental processes based upon a mind–body interaction paradigm. As we have seen, his focal point for such interactions was sexuality. In Part II we will elaborate on Freud's evolving concepts of the nature and role of sexuality in human development and the causation of neuroses. We will follow his developing theories of specific sexual causes for differentiated neurotic symptoms, as well as changes in his thinking about the deferred effects of early childhood experience on adult neuroses, in particular, his movement away from an emphasis on childhood sexual trauma to an emphasis on childhood sexual fantasy—the Oedipus complex and the determining power of unconscious-psychic reality. We will also track his changing methods of treatment for neuroses he believed had specific sexual etiologies, including his struggle with the power of suggestion in his therapeutic procedures. Of particular concern are the effects Freud's own sexual life had on his developing theories and how his bitter conflicts with Alfred Adler and C. G. Jung created motivations to revise his theories and issue new publications to defend his point of view in contrast to theirs. Some material presented in Part I is briefly repeated in Part II to maintain narrative coherence.

CHAPTER 9

J.-M. Charcot

While it is not possible to date exactly when the concepts of mental functioning which evolved into psychoanalytic theory first germinated in Freud's mind, the period from late 1885 to early 1886 was a major formative period in the birth of psychoanalysis. During this time, Freud, a twenty-nine-year-old Viennese neurologist, spent about four months in Paris studying with the renowned French neurologist J.-M. Charcot. He originally intended to pursue neurological studies. However, when he observed Charcot's clinical demonstrations in which hypnotic suggestion was used to produce paralysis in patients' limbs, his interest turned toward the clinical puzzle of hysteria. The paralyses caused by hypnotic suggestion were seen by Charcot as strikingly similar to some types of paralyses that occurred after railroad accidents, which, in the absence of observable neurological damage, Charcot attributed to post-traumatic psychological shock. Charcot reasoned that such post-traumatic cases of paralysis were caused by an autosuggestion of motor weakness, rooted in the mind during a self-induced hypnotic-like mental state, that occurred as a reaction to fear and shock. He further argued that *hysterical paralysis in general*, that is, any case of paralysis not traceable to specific organic damage, must be due to an autosuggestion implanted in the patient's mind during a self-induced, hypnotic-like mental state that was a spontaneous reaction to some *emotionally traumatic* experience. When patients regained normal consciousness, their autosuggestions of motor weakness remained active in a dissociated mental state as fixed ideas. This dissociated mental state was not accessible to ordinary consciousness. Nevertheless, these not consciously known autosuggested ideas of motor paralysis had the power to produce hysterical paralysis. According to Charcot (1882–1885), "the idea of motor paralysis," whether produced by hypnotism or by nervous shock, "that idea once installed in the brain takes sole possession and acquires sufficient domination to realize itself objectively in the form of paralysis" (p. 305).

Freud was profoundly influenced by Charcot. While he was in Paris he wrote to his fiancée: "Charcot, who is one of the greatest physicians and a man whose common sense borders on genius, is simply wrecking all my aims and opinions … no other human being has ever affected me in the same way" (in E. L. Freud, 1961, p. 196). On one occasion, according to Freud, a small group of students brought up on German academic physiology were trying Charcot's patience with doubts about his clinical innovations. Because some of his views contradicted a widely accepted theory, Freud provoked Charcot by exclaiming: "But that can't be true, it contradicts the Young–Helmholtz theory." Charcot responded to Freud's challenge with the iconic reply: "Theory is good, but it doesn't prevent things from existing"—which Freud claimed left "an indelible mark" upon his mind (Freud, 1893f, p. 13; see also Freud, 1925d, p. 13).

When he returned to Vienna in 1886, he was convinced that even in the absence of observable organic damage, hysterical paralyses and anesthesias were a genuine form of disease. Moreover, the cause of hysterical symptoms lay in the psychological realm: autosuggested ideas related to traumatic experiences could cause physical symptoms. Most importantly, in men as well as women, these autosuggested ideas that possessed causal efficacy were not part of ordinary conscious experience. In 1923, regarding the origins of psychoanalysis, Freud told Raymond Recouly: "The starting point … is to be found in Charcot's lessons at the Salpêtrière" (in Ruitenbeek, 1973, p. 59).

In 1886, Freud translated Charcot's clinical lectures on diseases of the nervous system (1882–1885) into German. The German version bore the title *New Lectures on Diseases of the Nervous System, Particularly on Hysteria.* Freud's German edition of Charcot's lectures, published in 1886, appeared before the French edition, which was first published in 1887.

For a history of concepts of hysteria and theoretical explanations for hysteria, see Micale (1995). For commentary on Freud's Paris experience with Charcot, see Gelfand (1992); for Charcot's influence on Freud's thinking about hysteria, see Freud (1956a), and Libbrecht and Quacklebeen (1995).

CHAPTER 10

Studies on hysteria

Before studying with Charcot, Freud had learned from an older Viennese physician, Josef Breuer, about his treatment of a young woman, Bertha Pappenheim, between 1880 and 1882. Bertha presented a variety of symptoms such as mental blackouts (absences), hallucinations, disturbances of sight and speech, muscular contractions and loss of feeling in arms and legs, nausea, and memory loss. Bertha evidenced a tendency, spontaneously, to enter trance-like or hypnoid mental states during which she reported stories and reveries. Based upon Breuer's then-unpublished written report on the case from 1882, it would appear that, at that time, Breuer told Freud that directing Bertha to narrate fantasies, reveries, and annoyances while in a trance-like state brought some relief from symptoms he believed were hysterical in nature (see the report in Hirschmüller (1978, pp. 276–290)). After his return from Paris, Freud began to apply the concepts of the psychical mechanisms of hysterical symptom formation he had learned from Charcot to an evolving new interpretation of the Bertha Pappenheim case.

In 1895, due to Freud's instigation, the volume *Studies on Hysteria*, by Freud and Breuer, was published. This volume contained a case history of Bertha Pappenheim, under the pseudonym of "Anna O."

The book also contained several other case histories of patients whom, by that time, Freud had treated for hysterical symptoms, as well as a Breuer chapter on theory and a Freud chapter on therapy. An 1893 preliminary communication concerning their views on psychical mechanisms in the causation of hysteria was included as the first chapter in the 1895 book that is often called the seminal book of psychoanalysis.

By the time of the publication of the 1893 preliminary communication, Freud had developed a point of view which differed markedly from Charcot's approach to hysteria. Breuer, on the other hand, maintained an opinion much like that of Charcot. Breuer accepted that entrance into a hypnoid state, in reaction to emotional trauma, was the prerequisite condition for traumatic memories, which were not available to ordinary consciousness, to become pathogenic roots of hysterical symptoms. Breuer's focus was on how undischarged nervous excitation, associated with a non-conscious traumatic memory, created an unbalanced energy distribution within the nervous system that contributed to hysterical symptom formation.

Contrary to Charcot and Breuer, by 1893 Freud saw no need to assume that an abnormal hypnoid mental state was involved in creating hysterical symptoms. As we have seen in Part I, he saw memories being excluded from consciousness and becoming pathogenic as a result of the patient being in conflict with the content of the memories. Such conflict arose because the memory content was incompatible with the patient's conscious view of self. The patient intentionally repressed or excluded from consciousness ideas that were incompatible with a positive conscious self-image, a psychical act of self-defense. According to Freud (1895d), "we have been led to the view that hysteria originates through the repression of an incompatible idea from a motive of defense" (Freud & Breuer, 1895d, p. 285). The previous year, Freud had stated: "In hysteria, the incompatible idea is rendered innocuous by its *sum of excitation being transformed into something somatic*. For this I should like to propose the name of *conversion*" (1894, p. 49, Freud's italics).

For Freud, in hysteria, psychic conflict over pathogenic memories involved defense and compromise formation. Nervous excitation associated with an incompatible idea embedded in a repressed memory was channeled into a somatic innervation that produced a physical symptom. This physical symptom was a compromise formation in that it now occupied a patient's consciousness in place of the incompatible idea which it symbolically represented, in a manner not consciously recognized—a poetic use of the body to represent, metaphorically, an unacceptable idea concerning one's self. For example: a self-threatening repressed memory of a scene containing the thought, "I can't bear to see this," could be represented physically as hysterical blindness; a remembered insult that was "too hard to swallow" might be represented physically as choking sensations. By the mid 1890s, he was convinced that the sum of excitation, the energy misdirected into the nervous system that was converted into a hysterical symptom, was sexual excitation that had been aroused in association with an incompatible repressed idea.

In *Studies on Hysteria*, Freud walked a diplomatic tightrope. Giving credit to Breuer's thesis, he accepted the possibility of the existence of hypnoid hysteria. "Strangely enough," he stated, "I have never in my own experience met with a genuine hypnoid hysteria." He was not able to suppress his belief "that somewhere or other the roots of hypnoid and defence hysteria come together, and that there the primary factor is defence. But I can say nothing about this" (p. 286).

In spite of his disagreements with Breuer, it was to Freud's advantage to publish jointly with him. A joint publication put the younger man in company with a highly respected physician and scientist, increasing the likelihood that his view would receive the acceptance that he desired.

Freud's belief that he was reporting significant discoveries concerning the cause and treatment of hysteria apparently helped him feel justified in encouraging Breuer to present what he knew was a false portrait of the Bertha Pappenheim (Anna O.) case—a presentation distorted to create, retrospectively, the myth that Anna O. was the primal psychoanalytic patient, the first patient to be cured of hysterical symptoms by a psychical treatment; in this case, a cathartic method claimed to be invented by Breuer. His discovery of a psychical mechanism and treatment in a case of hysteria was attributed to a date before publications on the role of traumatic memories in the causation of hysteria by Charcot, and the efficacy of using hypnosis to affect traumatic memories by Janet, Binet, and Delboeuf. A comparison of Breuer's notes on the Anna O. case from 1882, versus his 1895 published account, reveals a rewriting of the case history to now emphasize how the *emotional* narration of traumatic memories (not featured in the original report), recovered while Anna O. was in a self-induced hypnotic state, led to the cure of her hysterical symptoms (compare Freud & Breuer, 1895d, pp. 21–47) with Breuer (1882) in Hirshmüller (1978, pp. 276–290), and see Borch-Jacobsen (1996b) and Macmillan (1997, pp. 10–24).

Breuer and Freud claimed in 1895 that utilizing Anna O.'s self-induced hypnotic states, Breuer had successfully cured her hysterical symptoms by painstakingly tracing her symptoms back to forgotten emotional traumas. Once previously unavailable traumatic memories were recovered and narrated with full emotional expression, and associated suppressed nervous excitation which had been split off from them and become trapped in the nervous system was given an outlet through speech, the pathogenic memories were supposed to have been reunited with the split off "strangulated affect" and the symptoms connected to the pathogenic memories permanently removed. Breuer (1895d) stated: "from beginning to end of the illness all the stimuli arising from the secondary state, together with their consequences, were permanently removed by being given verbal utterance in hypnosis" (p. 46). But Breuer's "cures" of Bertha's hysterical symptoms were, for the most part, neither permanent nor complete.

Freud knew that a few weeks after Breuer terminated his treatment of Anna O. in 1882, she had to be hospitalized. While she was in the hospital (the Bellevue Sanatorium), she displayed serious relapses of symptoms Breuer had treated as hysterical. For example, mental blackouts (absences), hallucinations, and serious disturbances of speech and vision. Subsequently, between 1883 and 1887 Bertha had to be hospitalized at least three more times (see Ellenberger, 1972; Hirshmüller, 1978, pp. 112–116, 290–292). For a defense of Breuer's treatment of Anna O. see Skues (2006).

Over several decades there has been considerable speculation about what was "really" wrong with Anna O. (e.g., see Rosenbaum & Muroff, 1984). Peter Swales (1995) pointed out that "on termination of her treatment, Breuer's patient Anna O.—the subject of the legendary 'first case' of psychoanalysis—confessed that she had simulated her symptoms" (p. 107); (see Freud & Breuer, 1895d, p. 46; Hirschmüller, 1978, pp. 293, 295). Borch-Jacobsen (1996b) agreed that Anna O. had simulated her mysterious symptoms (pp. 83–92), but he concluded that her symptoms were not less real because they were simulated.

"On the contrary, they are *surreal* in the sense of simulation's being pushed to the point where the body goes along with it" (p. 91). It is possible that Anna O. intentionally manufactured or exaggerated some of her symptoms to keep the attention of her doctor, and, given his diagnosis of hysteria, it is possible that Anna O. behaved in a manner to meet her doctor's expectations for how a hysterical woman should behave. Anna O's hysteria may have been part of a role she played in a game with Breuer, "a game whose strange rules the two of them made up together as they went along" (Borch-Jacobsen, 1996b, p. 92). In this context, it is worth noting that Bertha refused to tell her stories to her hospital doctor, even when he asked much the same questions that Dr. Breuer had been asking during her treatment with him (see Hirschmüller, 1978, p. 287).

Mostly hidden in the 1895 published Anna O. case history is the fact that Breuer's treatment significantly turned Bertha into a drug addict. He repeatedly injected her with high doses of chloral hydrate and morphine (see documents in Hirchmüller, 1978, pp. 286–298; also see Ramos, 2003). Breuer (1895d) wrote that he "had been able to avoid the use of narcotics," for the most part (p. 30). Yet in a mid-June, 1882 letter to hospital doctor, Robert Binswanger, he reported that under his care, Bertha was

> receiving daily 0.08–0.1 morphine by injection … I am not engaged in breaking her of this addition [sic] since, despite her good will, when I am with her I am powerless to cope with her agitated state … for 1 year she has also received an evening dose of chloral … (In Hirschmüller, 1978, p. 293)

In this light it is probable that some of Anna O's diagnosed hysterical symptoms, before and after hospitalization, were, at least in part, reactions to high-level narcotics addiction, as well as signs of a drug-influenced mood disorder and narcotic affects upon brain functioning (see Ramos, 2003; Orr-Andrawes, 1987).

CHAPTER 11

Sexuality and neuroses

When Freud opened his practice as a neurologist in 1886, many gynecologists believed that hysteria was a female disease caused by anatomical changes and malfunctions of the female sexual and reproductive organs that affected the nervous system adversely (Porter, 1993; Bonomi, 1997). Therefore, surgery on those organs (see Dally, 2006) and/or clitoral stimulation, eventually utilizing electric vibrators to more efficiently produce a nervous energy release, a so-called "hysterical paroxysm," *rarely recognized as an orgasm* (!), were commonly prescribed (see Maines, 1999). In his first reported case history in *Studies on Hysteria*, Freud noted that in his treatment of "Frau Emmy Von N," "I shall massage her whole body twice a day" (1895d, p. 50). He did not mention whether the genital area was included as part of "her whole body."

The next twenty years saw an evolution of Freud's views on the role of sexuality in the neuroses. In 1888 he offered his opinion that, "As regards what is often asserted to be the preponderant influence of abnormalities in the sexual sphere upon the development of hysteria, it must be said that its importance is as a rule overestimated" (1888b, p. 50). He was challenging the prevailing gynecological view. He pointed out that hysteria also occurred in the male sex, in women who had lost their reproductive organs, and in woman whose sexual organs showed no morbid anatomical changes. "It must, however, be admitted," he stated, "that conditions related *functionally* to sexual life play a great part in the aetiology of hysteria (as of all neuroses), and they do so on account of the high psychical significance of this function especially in the female sex" (p. 51). Freud's focus here was on how difficulties in an adult's current sexual life affected the dynamics of excitation in the central nervous system, and how disturbances in the level of nervous excitation caused by misdirected, undischarged sexual excitation contributed to outbreaks of hysterical symptoms.

Freud's 1888 statement that hysteria depended on functional, rather than anatomical, sexual disorders was similar to earlier statements published in the 1860s by the Viennese neurologist, Moritz Benedikt, who Freud knew personally (see Ellenberger, 1970, 1973). In fact, it was Benedikt who had provided Freud with a handwritten letter of recommendation to present to Charcot upon his arrival in Paris in 1885.

Breuer saw sexuality playing no role in the Anna O. case; thus, in 1895 he would not go so far as to argue that *all* cases of hysteria had a sexual basis, a position which Freud would advocate. However, in *Studies on Hysteria* (1895d), Breuer did argue that: "The sexual instinct is undoubtedly the most powerful source of persisting increases in excitation (and consequently of neuroses). Such increases are distributed very unevenly over the nervous system" (p. 200). Therefore, according to Breuer, non-uniformly distributed excitation arising from the sexual emotion became converted into a hysterical bodily system.

Freud angrily ended his collaborations with Breuer in 1895. Years later, in 1907, Breuer recalled his collaboration with Freud in a letter to August Forel wherein Breuer stated that: "Together with Freud I was also able to observe the prominent place assumed by sexuality, and I can give an assurance that this arose from no inclination towards the subject but from the findings—to a large extend unexpected—of our medical experience" (in Cranefield, 1958, p. 320). However, recalling his resistance to Freud's evolving view that *all* cases of hysteria had a sexual basis, Breuer in 1907 stated: "Freud is a man given to absolute and exclusive formulations: this is a psychical need which, in my opinion, leads to excessive generalization" (in Cranefield, 1958, p. 320). In this regard, in 1894, while he was developing his view of the sexual basis of all neuroses, Freud told his confidant, the Berlin physician Wilhelm Fliess: "I am pretty much alone here in the elucidation of the neuroses. They look upon me as pretty much of a monomaniac, while I have the distinct feeling that I have touched upon one of the great secrets of nature" (in Masson, 1985, p. 74).

In *Studies on Hysteria* (1895d), Freud argued that: "As regards hysteria ... that disorder can scarcely be segregated from the nexus of sexual neuroses ... But an elucidation of these sexual neuroses would overstep the bounds of the present joint publication" (pp. 259, 261). He reserved for other publication his thoughts on the role of functional disturbances in the current sexual lives of adults in causing the actual neuroses (current neuroses): anxiety neuroses and neurasthenia, to be discusses below (see Freud, 1895b). In *Studies on Hysteria*, rather than focusing on the uneven distribution of excitation in the nervous system, he stressed his psychical-defense theory. Hysteria was a compromise formation, a defense against incompatible ideas and associated memories with sexual themes. These disturbing ideas and memories were secrets which the patient actively avoided acknowledging. Freud's focus was the elucidation of hidden unconscious motives which led to the nervous excitation, associated with the sexual content of repressed memories, being channeled (converted) into physical (hysterical) symptoms.

Concerning hysteria, Freud stated:

> it still strikes me myself as strange that the case histories I write should read like short stories and that, as one might say, they lack the serious stamp of science. I must console myself with the reflection that the nature of the subject is evidently responsible for this rather than any preference of my own ... a detailed description of mental processes such as we are accustomed to find in the works of imaginative writers enables me, with the use of a few psychological formulas, to obtain at least some kind of insight into the course of that affection. (Freud & Breuer, 1895d, pp. 160–161)

In *Studies on Hysteria*, Freud and Breuer (1895d) acknowledged some similarities (and differences) between their views on hysteria and those already published by Binet, Janet, and Delboeuf, as well as the views of some German speaking authors such as Moebius, Strümpell, and Benedikt (pp. 7, 8n.). Freud and Breuer stated that they found the nearest approach to their theoretical and therapeutic views in the work of Benedikt. He already had written about the pathogenic role of secrets relating to the patients' sexual life in cases of hysteria. In addition, he stressed the therapeutic value of guiding patients to a confession of their pathogenic secrets in a waking concentration state, without hypnosis, a procedure Freud increasingly utilized, starting in 1892, to be discussed below (see Andersson, 1962, pp. 114–116; Ellenberger, 1970, 1973).

In addition to defense neuroses which were psychogenic in origin such as hysteria and obsessional ideas, Freud (1895b) proposed that there were two actual neuroses—neuroses of organic origin—which definitely had a specific sexual basis: neurasthenia (a general weakness and fatigability) and anxiety neuroses (an overexcited condition). Each actual neurosis resulted from a failure to properly regulate the amount of internally produced sexual chemicals (hormones) in the bloodstream, through periodic, uninterrupted/climaxed sexual intercourse. Thus, the actual neuroses originated functionally in the current sexual life of the patient. In neurasthenia the sexual dysfunction was excessive masturbation which depleted the body of substances required for adequate internal excitation of the central nervous system. On the other hand, anxiety neurosis was an auto-toxic condition. It was the result of an accumulation of too much sexual chemistry, which overexcited the nervous system, producing anxiety. This neurosis was caused by sexual abstinence or coitus interruptus (withdrawal during sexual intercourse before ejaculation).

On March 1, 1896, Freud wrote to his confidant, the Berlin physician Wilhelm Fliess, that he regarded "the anxiety neurosis itself as an intoxication, for which an organic process must furnish the physiological foundation" (in Masson, 1985, p. 174). On April 16, 1896, he told Fliess: "I have always conceived of the processes in anxiety neuroses, as in the neuroses in general, as an intoxication, and often also thought of the similarity of the symptoms in anxiety neurosis and Basedow's disease ..." (in Masson, 1985, p. 180). Basedow's disease involves excessive production of thyroid secretion, which produces a rapid pulse and nervous symptoms. Knowledge of endocrine functions and chemistry was not well developed by the early 1890s (Castiglioni, 1958, pp. 806–808), but

Freud appeared to see analogies between discoveries of the second half of the nineteenth century concerning the effects of too much thyroid secretion (see Castiglioni, 1958, p. 781), and his hypothesized effects of too much internally produced sexual chemistry; both could be seen as auto-toxins which overly excited the nervous system.

Peter Swales (1983b) has argued that Freud's early experiments and personal experiences with the psychoactive properties of the alkaloid cocaine, during the 1880s and 1890s, probably influenced him in developing the belief that the adult body naturally produced sexual chemicals (analogous to the alkaloid) which produced sexual excitation, and which therefore had to be regulated through periodic, uninterrupted/climaxed sexual intercourse. In his 1884 paper, "Über Coca" ("On Cocaine"), Freud reported: "Among the persons to whom I have given coca, three reported violent sexual excitement which they unhesitatingly attributed to the coca" (in Byck, 1974, p. 73). On June 2, 1884, he wrote to his fiancée: "Woe to you, my princess, when I come, I will kiss you quite red and … you shall see who is the stronger, a gentle little girl who doesn't eat enough or a big wild man who has cocaine in his body" (Jones, 1953, p. 84).

Freud's theory that the specific causes of the actual neuroses were to be found in the current failure of adults to regulate properly their sexual chemistry through periodic, uninterrupted sexual intercourse most likely had a basis in his personal sex life. He was thirty years old when he married Martha Bernays in 1886 after a four-year-long engagement. He had hoped that, finally, marriage would at long last provide the sexual satisfaction he had so long been waiting for. As we have seen, however, on August 20, 1893, he confided to Wilhelm Fliess that in little more than six years of marriage, his wife had given birth to five children and, as a result, "we are now living in abstinence" (in Masson, 1985, p. 54). About fifteen years later, in an apparent autobiographical reflection, Freud (1908d) argued:

> satisfying sexual intercourse in marriage takes place only for a few years; and we must subtract from this, of course, the intervals of abstention necessitated by regard for the wife's health. After these three, four or five years, the marriage becomes a failure in so far as it has promised the satisfaction of sexual needs. For all

> the devices hitherto invented for preventing conception impair sexual enjoyment, hurt the fine susceptibilities of both partners and even actually cause illness. (p. 194)

Based in part on his personal experience, by 1895 Freud regarded prolonged sexual abstinence, or coitus interruptus, as causes for anxiety neurosis. During the fall of 1893, during the period when he was not enjoying sexual intercourse with his wife, he began to complain of cardiac symptoms which could be features of anxiety neuroses. These symptoms reached a peak in spring 1894 when Freud complained of "violent arrhythmia" and "constant tension" (in Masson, 1985, p. 67). Fliess diagnosed Freud's cardiac symptoms as the result of toxic effects of nicotine, caused by his addiction to cigar smoking. Subsequently, in December 1897, perhaps in a moment of unacknowledged self-reference concerning how he struggled to cope with continuing sexual frustration, Freud told Fliess that he believed that all addictions, such as to tobacco, were substitutions for the "primary addiction" of habitual masturbation (in Masson, 1985, p. 287).

Jones (1953) argued that Freud's cardiac symptoms "were in the main special aspects of his psychoneuroses, possibly slightly localized by the effect of nicotine" (p. 311). Schur (1972), on the other hand, offered the opinion that Freud's cardiac symptoms were of organic origin (p. 62). Regardless of the cause of Freud's heart issues, because he regarded the then-available methods of birth control as distasteful and harmful and he wished to spare himself and his wife from a continuing succession of child-following-child, he was forced to live with an accumulating unfulfilled sexual desire within his marriage. He associated it with his tendency toward significant mood swings and his felt need to sublimate his sexual drive. In October, 1897, at age forty-one, he told Fliess: "Sexual excitement ... is no longer of use for someone like me" (in Masson, 1985, p. 276). In March, 1900, he told Fliess: "You know how limited my pleasures are ... I am done begetting children ..." (in Masson, 1985, p. 404).

It is likely that some of Freud's late-nineteenth-century patients experienced marital-sexual discontents similar to those that troubled him, and that he increasingly assumed that they did and sought to unmask sexual secrets (including excessive masturbation) and secrets of the marriage-bed through the queries he directed toward his patients. In this regard, it is worth noting that in his 1907 recollection of his collaboration with Freud, Breuer remarked that among their patients, "sexual abnormalities (coitus interruptus), etc." frequently were found to stand in causal relationship to neurotic symptoms (in Cranefield, 1958, p. 319).

Freud (1914d) reported that in the early 1880s, Breuer had remarked to him—concerning a neurotic patient of Breuer's: "[T]hese things are always *secrets d'alcove!*" (secrets of the marriage-bed) (p. 13). Further, he stated (1914d) that, subsequently, he had heard similar remarks concerning certain neurotic symptoms made by Charcot and the Viennese gynecologist Chrobak (pp. 13–15). Thus, while in 1914 Freud reported that during the 1880s other physicians he respected had known that certain neurotic symptoms had a functional sexual basis, retrospectively he accused them of being too hesitant to publish their secret knowledge for fear of offending the then-current standards of civil discourse. During the 1890s, he increasingly became obsessed with the mission of revealing and elaborating systematically what he believed were the specific sexual causes of all neurotic symptoms, even if this seemed to shock bourgeois sensibilities, and to put him in opposition to the manners of polite society (see Cuddihy, 1974, pp. 89–97).

Freud was encouraged to speculate about the role of sexual physiology in the neuroses by his frequent correspondent, Wilhelm Fliess. His letters to Fliess during the 1890s document the development of his thinking during this period (see Masson, 1985). Both men drew on the 1884 work of George Miller Beard, *Sexual Neurasthenia*, which proposed that one of the causes of neurasthenia was an expenditure of "nerve force" which could be caused by frequent masturbation (see Bunker, 1930; Macmillan, 1997, pp. 121–131). Many late-nineteenth-century physicians saw habitual masturbation as related to a damaged nervous system, as cause or effect. For example, Schrenk-Notzing (1892) stated:

> According to the later psychiatric investigations (Christian, Kraepelin, Vogel, Löwenfeld, Uffelmann, Krafft-Ebing, etc.) it is put beyond doubt that habitual masturbation is either a concomitant symptom of an existent neuropathic condition, or as a rule, induces, in connection with inherited or acquired predisposition, pronounced disturbances of the nervous system. (p. 7)

Many doctors at this time attributed primary importance to frequent masturbation as a cause of neurasthenia, among them Krafft-Ebing, Erb, Rohleder, and Leyden (see Ellis, 1910, p. 260). While in the late nineteenth century it was the case that many physicians linked masturbation with neurasthenia, Freud (1895b) boldly claimed that excessive masturbation was the *one specific cause* for this actual neurosis (although, in his *Introductory Lectures on Psycho-Analysis* (1916–17) he stated: "Even at that time I could not fail to notice that the causation of the illness did not always point to sexual life" (p. 386).)

In sum, by 1896, Freud argued that *all neuroses were sexual in origin*. The *defense neuroses*, hysteria, obsessional neuroses, and phobias, were ideogenic. He now reasoned that the defense neuroses were compromise formations employed in defending against excessively intense memories that were associatively connected to early traumatic sexual experiences (to be discussed below as "the seduction theory"). Psychical conflict over the content of post-pubertal memories, associatively linked to early sexual traumas, prevented proper discharge of the nervous excitation associated with the memories. This nervous energy took a wrong turn into hysterical physical symptoms, or this energy was channeled through psychical pathways to produce excessively intense obsessional ideas or phobic thoughts. *The actual neuroses* were the outcome of imbalances of internally produced sexual chemicals, affecting the level of excitation in the nervous system, resulting from functional disturbances in an adult's current sexual life (see Levin, 1978; Silverstein, 1985, 2003; May, 1999).

By 1896, Freud not only differentiated several types of neurotic symptoms descriptively: anxiety neurosis, neurasthenia, hysteria, and obsessional neurosis, but unlike most writers on neurosis before him, he attempted a unifying explanatory framework which traced each type of neurosis to a specific pathological etiology which was the cause of the symptoms. For Freud, the specific cause of each type of neurosis was to be found in sexuality, conceived in both physical and psychical terms. He (1896a) stated:

> Sexual disorders have always been admitted among the causes
> of nervous illness, but they have been subordinated to hered-
> ity and co-ordinated with the other *agents provocateurs*; their
> aetiological influence has been restricted to a limited number of

observed cases … what gives its distinctive character to my line of approach is that I elevate these sexual influences to the rank of specific causes, that I recognize their action in every case of neurosis, and finally that I trace a regular parallelism, a proof of a special aetiological relation between the nature of the sexual influence and the pathological species of the neurosis. (p. 149)

Freud believed that improperly discharged sexual excitation (energy) produced by the body's sexual physiology was at the root of the physical and mental symptoms of the neuroses. He argued (1905e):

Some of my colleagues have looked upon my theory of hysteria as a purely psychological one … It is the therapeutic technique alone that is purely psychological; the theory does not by any means fail to point out that neuroses have an organic basis … No one, probably will be inclined to deny the sexual function the character of an organic factor, and it is the sexual function that I look upon as the foundation for hysteria and of the psychoneuroses in general. No theory of sexual life will, I suspect, be able to avoid assuming the existence of some definite sexual substances having an excitant action. (p. 113)

In 1908 Freud told Jung: "In the sexual processes we have the indispensable 'organic foundation' without which a medical man can only feel ill at ease in the life of the psyche" (in McGuire, 1974, pp. 140–141).

Freud's creation of a unifying scheme for classifying neuroses and his search for specific causes for specific symptoms were influenced by the great advances in bacteriology and the rise of germ theory in the last half of the nineteenth century (see Carter, 1980). Great progress had been made in understanding how a particular microorganism such as the tubercle bacillus was involved in causing a certain infectious disease, tuberculosis (see Castiglioni, 1958, pp. 809–829). Freud saw analogies between the necessary precondition that specific infectious diseases could not occur without exposure to specific germs, such that tuberculosis could not occur without exposure to the tuberculosis bacillus, and his proposed necessary preconditions and specific causes for each type of neurosis, which had to be present in every case (see Freud, 1896c, p. 209).

Thus, he saw childhood sexual traumas as the necessary precondition, and post-pubertal conflicts and defenses over excessively intense memories of such experiences as the specific causes for particular defense neuroses—hysteria and obsessional ideas. He also saw specific current adult sexual practices and sexual toxins as the specific causes for the actual neuroses—neurasthenia and anxiety neurosis. In 1896, Freud's search for specific causes for hysteria and obsessional neurosis was focusing on how differentially experienced, or timed, childhood sexual traumas served as the necessary preconditions for these disorders, and how the post-pubertal transformation and repression of memories of such experiences was a specific cause for the appearance of the symptoms of these disorders after puberty had been achieved; his "seduction theory" below.

CHAPTER 12

From hypnosis to "pressure"

The development of Freud's method of psychotherapy is inextricably bound to the evolution of his psychological theories. In 1887, he was using hypnotic suggestion as a mode of therapy. From 1889 he combined hypnotic suggestion with hypnotic searching for the narration of traumatic memories; at this time, he was trying to remove the excessive excitation of traumatic memories through hypnotic suggestions (see Swales, 1986 and Macmillan, 1997, pp. 69–114). From 1892, he used suggestive directed concentration in the waking state to try to access repressed pathogenic ideas, and associated traumatic memories, whose intensity might be relieved through conscious emotionally charged narration.

Between 1892 and 1895, Freud had begun using his "pressure technique" as a way to access pathogenic ideas and associated traumatic memories from patients who were resistant to hypnosis. In *Studies on Hysteria*, he explained (1895d):

> I told the patients to lie down and deliberately close their eyes in order to "concentrate" … I inform the patient that, a moment later, I shall apply pressure to his forehead, and I assure him that,

> all the time the pressure lasts, he will see before him a recollection
> in the form of a picture or will have it in his thoughts in the form
> of an idea occurring to him … (p. 270)

The patient was instructed to communicate to Freud whatever came to mind under the stimulation of his "pressure." It was his hope that under his "pressure" an image associatively linked to a core-repressed pathogenic idea would emerge. By continuous repetition of this procedure, he would follow a chain of associations which enabled him to *infer* a core-repressed incompatible idea. He then told the patient what he believed the repressed pathogenic idea was, and he directed the patient to accept his interpretation and to engage in an emotional verbal expression of the pathogenic memory and associated pathogenic idea to discharge the excessive excitation associated with them. This procedure was supposed to remove the symptom that symbolically represented the repressed incompatible idea as a compromise formation.

Freud's "pressure technique" was based upon observations he had made in 1889. Trying to improve his skills as a hypnotist he had returned to France, but this time to Nancy, to study with H. Bernheim, an advocate for the therapeutic use of hypnosis (see Bernheim, 1887; Forrest, 1999, pp. 213–253). Bernheim insisted that hypnosis was simply suggestion and was not related to any pathological mental state, as Charcot had argued. Bernheim taught Freud that relaxing a patient and insisting that the patient recall some event, seemingly unavailable to consciousness, produced the desired recollection without hypnosis. By 1895, following Bernheim's lead, Freud had created his "pressure technique."

In 1896, Freud used the term "psycho-analysis" for the first time to refer to the directed, waking-concentration method he was using then (including the "pressure technique") to trace hysterical symptoms back to their origin in repressed incompatible ideas, associated with repressed traumatic memories. This procedure aimed at the therapeutic reduction of the excessively intense excitation associated with the repressed memories through the cathartic narration and emotional expression of the traumatic emotionally charged memories, and the incompatible ideas associated with them (see 1896a, p. 151).

CHAPTER 13

The seduction theory

Even though by 1895 Freud had separated himself from Charcot and Breuer, he still was guided by the then medically current trauma theory to search for a specific actual traumatic event which overstimulated the nervous system as the necessary precondition for the development of hysteria (see Makari, 1998). In conceptualizing the nature of a traumatic event which could serve as the necessary precondition for hysteria, by 1895 he had begun to formulate what would become known as his "seduction theory," the idea that the post-pubertal *repression of memories* which had become traumatic concerning shocking *childhood sexual abuse experiences* was a necessary cause in the formation of hysterical symptoms. On October 8, 1895, he told Fliess, "I am on the scent of the following strict precondition for hysteria, namely that a primary sexual experience [before puberty], accompanied by revulsion and fright, must have taken place; for obsessional neurosis, that it must have happened, accompanied by pleasure" (in Masson, 1985, p. 141). On October 15, he repeated his great "clinical secret" to Fliess: "Hysteria is the consequence of a presexual *sexual* shock" (in Masson, 1985, p. 144)

In 1895, Freud had not yet developed his concept of childhood sexuality; at this time, he thought of sexuality as a function which began with the arrival of puberty. Therefore, he reasoned that stimulation of a young child's genitals would be a shocking, overstimulating, traumatic experience for the child. However, it was not childhood sexual abuse experiences per se that caused adult defense neuroses; the cause of such neuroses was the *deferred action* of memories of such experiences which were *retranscripted*, that is, first given sexual meanings after puberty had been achieved. In the post-pubertal period, hysterical and obsessional patients came into conflict with the new sexual meanings that they now attributed to the memories of their much earlier childhood experiences, and their hysterical and obsessional symptoms were the product of their defenses against such newly sexualized memories and thoughts associatively linked to them which now became excessively exciting. Freud (1895) reasoned that "Here we have the case of a memory arousing an affect which it did not arouse as an experience, because in the meantime the change [brought about] in puberty had made possible a different understanding of what was remembered" (1950a, p. 356).

Noting that the *adult* experiences associated with the appearance of hysterical symptoms often seemed not sufficiently traumatic to cause neurosis, he (1896c) argued that: "We have learned that *no hysterical symptom can arise from a real experience alone, but that in every case the memory of earlier experiences awakened in association to it plays a part in causing the symptom*" (p. 197, Freud's italics). Further, he stated (1896c):

> We must rather ask ourselves: where shall we get to if we follow the chain of associated memories which the analyst has uncovered? ... Whatever case and whatever symptom we take as our point of departure, *in the end we infallibly come to the field of sexual experience.* (p. 100, Freud's italics)

Where did the chain of memories finally lead? Freud claimed that the chain of memories inevitably led back to early childhood experiences of sexual abuse: he therefore argued "that at the bottom of every case of hysteria there are *one or more occurrences of premature sexual experience*, occurrences which belong to the earliest years of childhood but which can be reproduced through the work of psycho-analysis in spite of the intervening decades" (p. 203, Freud's italics).

Over a period of almost two years, Freud's speculations concerning shocking sexual events which must have occurred when his adult patients were children appeared to be confirmed as his patients, if often with expressions of disbelief in response to his directed waking concentration and "pressure technique," obliged him by telling him stories or acquiescing to his reconstructions which fit his current version of a suspected necessary precondition for hysteria. The blame for the prepubertal sexual abuse, which must have happened, shifted several times as he reformulated his etiological hypothesis. First, older children were most often blamed as abusers; then suspicion increasingly shifted to adult caretakers or strangers. Finally, even though he had *not* made this statement in his publications, in September 1897 he told Fliess that he had concluded that in all cases it was the *father* who "had to be accused of being perverse" (in Masson, 1985, p. 264), although he told Fliess that he found it difficult to accept the implication that father-initiated sexual abuse of children was as frequent as were cases of hysteria. Nevertheless, guided by his suggestions and his "pressure," his patients, if often grudgingly, may have submitted in some manner in corroborating childhood sexual abuse stories which matched his current speculation concerning a necessary shocking childhood sexual event, the memory of which could generate distressing emotions in the post-pubertal period because new sexual meaning had now been attributed to the memory.

The suggestive nature of Freud's method for extracting what he believed were repressed memories of childhood sexual abuse from his patients is apparent in his statements from the period when he developed his seduction theory. In *Studies on Hysteria*, he stated (1895d): "We need not be afraid ... of telling the patient what we think his next connection of thought is going to be. It will do no harm" (p. 295). He stated that before he applied his analytic procedure his patients claimed to have no memories of being sexually abused in childhood:

> They are indignant as a rule if we warn them that such scenes are going to emerge. Only the strongest compulsion of the treatment can induce them to embark on a reproduction of them ... and even after they have gone through them ... in such a convincing manner, they still attempt to withhold belief from them

> by emphasizing the fact that unlike what happens in the case of
> other forgotten material, they have no feeling of remembering
> the "scenes." (p. 204)

When his patients claimed to have no memories of having been sexually abused as children, he appeared to see such denials as proof that the
memories of such experiences had become so traumatic that they were
repressed.

In 1896, Freud insisted that, in spite of his patients' apparent refusals
to accept the validity of the sexual abuse memories he believed his analytic procedure had uncovered, he did not believe that he had forced such
stories upon his patients, nor had his patients obliged him by inventing
fictitious stories. Rhetorically, he argued (1896c): "I have never yet succeeded in forcing on a patient a scene I was expecting to find, in such a
way that he seemed to be living through it with all the appropriate feelings" (p. 205). And, "Why should patients assure me so emphatically of
their unbelief, if what they want to discredit is something which—from
whatever motive—they themselves have invented?" (p. 204). However,
in spite of the resistance and denials that his patients offered, in 1896 he
believed that recovering traumatic childhood sexual abuse memories in
the context of a memory affirming cathartic emotional experience, was
an absolute requirement to cure psychogenic defense neuroses.

In two papers Freud sent for publication in February 1896, he claimed
to have carried out "a complete psycho-analysis" in thirteen cases of hysteria, with each case revealing early sexual traumas (see 1896a, p. 152).
In April 1896, he gave a lecture on his seduction theory. A written version of this lecture, "The Aetiology of Hysteria," was mailed for publication at the end of May. In it he put forth the thesis that at the bottom
of every case of hysteria there were single or multiple occurrences of
premature sexual experiences, dating from the earliest years. He now
claimed (1896c) that "in some eighteen cases of hysteria I have been
able to discover this connection in every single symptom, and where
the circumstances allowed, to confirm it by *therapeutic success*" (p. 199).

Barely sixteen months after Freud's bold claims for confirmation and
therapeutic success, on September 21, 1897, he wrote to Fliess: "I no
longer believe in my *neurotica*," that is, his seduction theory. Further
the first reason he offered for his change of mind was "the continual

disappointment in my efforts to bring a single analysis to a real conclusion; ... the absence of the complete successes on which I had counted; the possibility of explaining to myself the partial success in other ways, in the usual fashion" (in Masson, 1985, p. 264). What is apparent here is that in private communication to Fliess, Freud indicated that he had *not* achieved the *permanent* or *complete therapeutic success* with his patients suggested in his publications of the previous year. Furthermore, his 1897 understanding that he could explain his "partial successes" in "the usual fashion" suggests that, despite his earlier denials, now he could not rule out the possibility that his patients were responding to his suggestions (or autosuggestions) and his "pressure" when they obliged him by acquiescing to reconstructions which fit his etiological hypothesis of the moment. As his critics had been charging, the childhood scenes he claimed his patients had been reporting, for the most part, came from him; additionally, his "psycho-analysis" could be seen as just a form of Bernheim's "suggestible therapeutics" (see Borch-Jacobsen, 1996a).

As much as he recognized the role that suggestion might have played in shaping his patients' behavior toward confirming his expectations concerning his seduction theory, he always backed away from publicly acknowledging that his suggestions were the source of patients' sexual abuse stories. Although Freud (1925d) retrospectively stated that in 1897, "I was at last obliged to recognize that these scenes of seduction had never taken place, and that they were only phantasies which my patients had made up or which I myself had perhaps forced on them ...," a few sentences later he pulled back from an apparent admission of the role his suggestions played in shaping his patients' behavior by insisting: "I do not believe even now that I forced the seduction-phantasies on my patients, that I 'suggested' them" (p. 34).

To defend his earlier claims that his patients had reported scenes of childhood sexual abuse, and that such stories were not simply the product of his suggestions, in his September 21, 1897 letter to Fliess he went on to conjecture: "there would remain the solution that the sexual fantasy invariably seizes upon the theme of the parents," and "there are no indications of reality in the unconscious," so that in the unconscious "one cannot distinguish between truth and fiction ..." and in analysis, "the unconscious never overcomes the resistance of the conscious" (in Masson, 1985, pp. 264–265). Here is the start of a major turning point in the development of psychoanalytic theory.

Freud side-stepped the dilemma of suggestion and he protected his theories of psychic-conflict, repression, and defense neuroses by speculating that he actually had succeeded in unearthing derivatives of repressed material from his patients' unconscious minds associated with early sexual trauma. However, what was repressed were childhood *sexual fantasies* that expressed sexual wishes concerning the parents, perhaps associated with fantasy-driven, overstimulating, traumatic childhood masturbation (see Makari, 1998). These childhood sexual fantasies were experienced as reality in the unconscious, and they never overcame repression, emerging in consciousness only as derivative, defensive, compromise-formation memories of parental sexual abuse (and with later theoretical development, as disguised fulfilled wishes in dreams). In other words, Freud continued to assert that his patients had reported childhood sexual abuse scenes, and the sexual abuse scenes were internal productions that originated in his patients' minds; they were constructions that the patients defensively created to mask the reality of repressed childhood *sexual fantasies*, wishes, and autoerotic practices which the abuse scenes symbolically represented. Over the next several years, he developed his new concept of repressed childhood sexual wishes and fantasies concerning parents into his concept of the Oedipus complex.

Looking back on his 1896c paper in which he proclaimed the seduction theory, in 1924 he added a footnote to that early paper: "at the time I wrote it I had not yet freed myself from my *overevaluation* of reality and my *low evaluation* of phantasy" (1924d, p. 204, n.1, Freud's italics). As his views evolved, he argued that even though

> the patient has created these phantasies for himself, … this fact is of scarcely less importance for his neurosis than if he had really experienced what the phantasies contain. The phantasies possess *psychical* as contrasted with *material* reality, and we gradually learn to understand that *in the world of the neuroses* it is psychical reality which is the decisive kind. (1916–17, p. 368, Freud's italics)

He never denied that actual sexual abuse of children occurred or that it produced harmful psychological effects. But for the *psychoneuroses*, he saw repressed fantasies and wishes, the *psychical reality* as the necessary determining factor.

With the abandonment of his seduction theory, Freud no longer saw the first acts of repression as a post-pubertal event—he now believed that the repressions of sexual wishes and fantasies concerning parents took place in early childhood. In 1915 and 1926, as we have seen, he distinguished between the first repressions of sexual wishes in early childhood which he called "primal repression," and later repressions of derivatives of primal repressed wishes which he called "repression proper."

In the fall of 1897, he increasingly speculated on a point only suggested the year before: children have a sexual life before puberty, even in early childhood, which decisively influenced later sexual development. His concept of childhood sexuality, which developed over several years from 1897 to 1905, derived in part from suggestions he accepted from Wilhelm Fliess, as well as from the writings of some late-nineteenth-century pediatricians and prominent sexologists, such as Albert Moll and Havelock Ellis. (See Kern, 1973; Sulloway, 1979, pp. 277–319; Carter, 1983; Gilman, 1994; and Bonomi, 1997). However, by 1905, in Freud's hands the concept of childhood sexuality would be elaborated, differentiated, and linked to later adult characteristics in a unique, systematic fashion. By 1905 he no longer conceptualized childhood masturbation itself as traumatic and pathogenic. He reconceptualized childhood self-stimulating masturbation as a pregenital expression of an innate sexual drive that evolved through stages, affecting various erogenous zones from infancy to puberty.

For varying commentaries on Freud's seduction theory see M. I. Klein (1981), Swales (1982b, 1983a), Schimek (1987), Frampton (1991), Israëls and Schatzman (1993), Salyard (1994), Borch-Jacobsen (1996a), and Macmillan (1997, pp. 206–229).

CHAPTER 14

Fragments of Freud's self-analysis

In 1896, Freud's father died. Freud experienced significant emotional stress in coping with this death and, as a result, began to apply his evolving psychoanalytic method to himself—he started a process of self-analysis. At first, he looked for evidence of childhood sexual abuse in his own case, even possibly involving his father. However, after he repudiated his theory that actual childhood sexual abuse was the necessary precondition required in every case of hysteria, he examined his own childhood for evidence of repressed sexual wishes that would corroborate his new hypothesis. On October 3, 1897, he reported to Fliess that when he was a young boy his "libido toward *matrem*" was awakened during a railway journey he took with his mother, "during which we must have spent the night together and there must have been an opportunity of seeing her *nudam*" (in Masson, 1985, p. 268). These were not actual memories, but reconstructions of what must have happened to provide data that would support his new theory.

Less than two weeks later on October 15, he wrote to Fliess:

> A single idea of general value dawned on me. I have found, in
> my own case too, [the phenomenon of] being in love with my

mother and jealous of my father, and I now consider it a universal event in early childhood, even if not so early as in children who have been made hysterical. (In Masson, 1985, p. 272)

Now, based on his *interpretive reconstructions* of his patients' and his own childhood, he made the theoretical leap that *all children* experienced a sexualized love for the mother, and jealousy of the father, the precursor of what in 1910 he officially named the "Oedipus complex" (see Freud, 1910h, p. 171).

CHAPTER 15

The dilemma of suggestion

Freud's reported *discoveries*, first of repressed memories of childhood sexual abuse, and second of repressed childhood sexual wishes and fantasies, were largely based on his search for retrospective material concerning childhood which he could interpret as consistent with the hypothesis he already had in hand. In other words, he repeatedly found what he expected to find: his clinical data always showed him what his hypothesis predicted. While by definition subjective interpretations of the contents of another person's mind, or his own mind, cannot meet a standard of objective clinical data collection and hypothesis testing, nevertheless, Freud regarded his ability to find clinical data which he could *interpret* as supporting his theories as genuine scientific validation of his theories. He believed that if he could induce his patients to accept the validity of his interpretations of the hidden symbolic meanings of their thoughts and symptoms, such acceptance validated his theoretical premises and made his interpretations "facts." Additionally, he believed that if he could extract confessions from his patients concerning sexual practices and experiences that he believed were causally related to their symptoms, such confessions gave truth-value to his specific causal hypotheses.

Here are some examples of Freud's manner of seeking validation for his theoretical preconceptions and causal hypotheses. In *Studies on Hysteria*, he defended the use of his pressure technique to extract from a patient what he had already hypothesized was the correct pathogenic idea and traumatic memory which lay at the root of his patient's hysterical symptoms. He stated:

> It is remarkable how often patients … can completely forget their undertaking … They promise to say whatever occurred to them under the pressure of my hand … But they do not keep this promise … they keep on maintaining that this time nothing has occurred to them. We must not believe what they say … we must repeat the pressure and represent ourselves as infallible … The principal point is that I should guess the secret and tell it to the patient straight out; and he is then as a rule obliged to abandon his rejection of it. (Freud & Breuer, 1895d, pp. 279, 281)

In 1897, when writing to Fliess concerning a female patient who, in his judgment must have suffered childhood sexual abuse by her father, Freud stated:

> When I thrust the explanation at her, she was at first won over … She is now in the throes of the most vehement resistance … I have threatened to send her away and in the process convinced myself that she has already gained a good deal of certainty which she is reluctant to acknowledge. (In Masson, 1985, pp. 220–221)

The following statement gives us another glimpse of Freud's manner of validating his clinical theory. Once he had diagnosed cases of neurasthenic neurosis, armed with his conception of its cause lying in the masturbatory sexual practices of his adult patients, he stated (1898a):

> we may then boldly demand confirmation of our suspicions from the patient. We must not be led astray by initial denials. If we keep firmly to what we have inferred, we shall in the end conquer every resistance by emphasizing the unshakeable nature of our convictions. (p. 269)

Even after abandonment of the seduction theory in 1898 he still kept pressuring patients to confirm the correctness of his causal hypotheses and interpretations, and he appeared to see his role as overcoming patients' resistance to accepting the validity of his views. In his *Introductory Lectures on Psycho-Analysis*, Freud (1916–17) reported how he had pressured neurasthenic patients to confirm his hypothesis concerning their sexual practices: "I also learnt then to stand obstinately by my suspicions till I had overcome the patients' disingenuousness and compelled them to confirm my views" (p. 386).

While it might be argued that the above examples represent Freud in a pre-psychoanalytic period, that is, before the year 1900, his five post-1900 published case histories reveal that he continued to pressure patients to accept the validity of his constructions concerning pathogenic early childhood events, and the content of their repressions, as well as his interpretations of the symbolic meanings of their dreams and psychoneurotic symptoms. This can be seen in Freud's reported cases such as "Dora" (1905e) and "The Rat Man" (1909d). See Sulloway (1992) for reassessments of Freud's case histories. In the "Dora" case, Freud explained that when his interpretations of a patient's repressed thoughts were strongly rejected by the patient,

> [t]he "No" uttered by a patient after a repressed thought has been presented to his conscious perception for the first time does no more than register the existence of a repression and its severity; it acts, as it were, as a gauge of the repression's strength. If this "No", instead of being regarded as the expression of an impartial judgement (of which, indeed, the patient is incapable), is ignored, and if the work is continued, the first evidence soon begins to appear that in such a case "No" signifies the desired "Yes." (pp. 58–59)

Freud used the suggestive impact of his personality and his growing fame to induce his patients to develop an emotionally dependent relationship toward him and, in that context, to accept his belief system as a guide for a curative process. In this regard, see Roazen (1995) for revealing interviews with some of Freud's later psychoanalytic patients. He required his patients to develop a religious-like faith in him and his belief system, and his successful therapeutic outcomes had elements of religious conversion experiences. Perhaps it is not coincidental that the late nineteenth and early twentieth centuries were a period of intense religious revivalist movements (see S. M. Silverstein, 1988). In the early decades of the twentieth century Freud's psychoanalysis became, in effect, a secular religious movement with him being seen by many as a godlike figure.

CHAPTER 16

From suggestion to transference

As Freud progressively abandoned reliance on therapeutic hypnosis in 1892, he began to employ the method of directed free association in response to some patients' protestations that he should let them talk. He did start to listen to what his patients had to say. Nevertheless, he still relied on the pressure technique and directed waking concentration. With the collapse of his seduction theory, he claimed to make free association his fundamental method for gathering clinical data, since he believed that free association avoided the pitfall of the appearance of the therapists' suggestions determining what the patient reported. With free association, he observed that patients sometimes resisted following his directive to report uncensored whatever came to mind. He interpreted such resistance as evidence for repression and made analysis and interpretation of such resistance a fundamental part of his (non-hypnosis based) psychoanalytic technique.

Even after abandoning hypnotic and pressure techniques, he remained concerned with an explanation for suggestion itself—how and why might a patient become vulnerable to meeting demands (even if inadvertent) from a therapist? As we have seen, as early as 1890 (1890a, p. 296), he had speculated that a hypnotized person adopted a relationship to a hypnotist such as shown only by a child to a parent (see Silverstein & Silverstein, 1990, for a review of Freud's attempts to explain the power of suggestion). His adoption of the concept of childhood sexual desire for the parent enabled him to propose a new explanation for the power of suggestion (or autosuggestion) in his work with his patients. He spoke of an unconscious fixation of the subjects' sexual desire (libido) to the figure of the hypnotist, as though the hypnotist were the parent (Freud, 1905d, p. 150). In addition, he used the term "transference" (1905e) to refer to the necessity for the arousal in the analytic patient of impulses and fantasies concerning parents which the patient directed toward the analyst, even though no hypnosis was employed. He concluded that: "it is only after the transference has been resolved that a patient arrives at a sense of conviction of the validity of the connections which have been constructed during the analysis" (pp. 116–117). In his *Introductory Lectures on Psycho-Analysis*, he (1916–17) stated: "in our technique we have abandoned hypnosis only to rediscover suggestion in the shape of transference" (p. 446).

For Freud, transference referred to the actual expression of unconscious wishes in a specific relationship. He believed that in the analytic situation, a patient's childhood sexual and aggressive wishes reemerged, focused on the analyst, and were experienced with a vivid sensation of immediacy. Not just the surfacing of previously unacknowledged childhood wishes, but the achievement of insight, acceptance, and the working through of such wishes, through interpretation and resolution of the transference, came to define the nature of a psychoanalytic cure.

Why should a patient accept the correctness of Freud's interpretations concerning their resistance and transference of repressed childhood sexual wishes toward the analyst? According to him (1926e), the neurotic patient developed faith in the correctness of the analyst's interpretations,

> because he acquires a special emotional attitude towards the figure of the analyst … this emotional relation is, to put it plainly, in the nature of falling in love (pp. 224–225) … The patient is *repeating* in the form of falling in love with the analyst, mental experiences which he has already been through *once* before; he has *transferred* on to the analyst mental attitudes that were lying

ready in him and were intimately connected with his neurosis. He is also repeating ... his old defensive actions; he would like best to repeat in his relation to the analyst *all* the history of that forgotten period of his life ... *he is reproducing it tangibly as though it were actually happening, instead of remembering it.* (pp. 226–227, Freud's italics)

He used a patient's desire to please the analyst (to win the analyst's love) as a catalyst to move a patient toward acceptance of the correctness of his interpretations. With his concept of transference, he conceptualized a way in which he could make use of the erotic quality of suggestion to overcome patients' resistance to accepting the correctness of his interpretations concerning the hidden meanings of their emotional conflicts, and the specific causes of their symptoms.

Freud never stopped being concerned with the dilemma of suggestion. If positive transference toward the analyst influenced patients to accept the validity of his suggestions concerning the nature of their repressions and the meaning of their symptoms, how could he be sure that his interpretations accurately reflected the content of a patient's unconscious mind? In his *Introductory Lectures on Psycho-Analysis* (1916–17), he considered this dilemma: "But now you will tell me that, no matter whether we call the motive force of our analysis transference or suggestion, there is a risk that the influencing of our patients may make the objective certainty of our findings doubtful" (p. 452). In his defense he asserted that even though his critics charged

that we have "talked" the patients into everything relating to the importance of sexual experiences ... Anyone who has himself carried out psycho-analyses will have been able to convince himself on countless occasions that it is impossible to make suggestions to patients in that way. The doctor has no difficulty, of course, in making him a supporter of some particular theory and in thus making him share some possible error of his own ... but this only affects his intelligence, not his illness. After all, his conflicts will only be successfully solved and his resistances overcome if the anticipatory ideas he is given *tally* with what is real in him. (p. 452)

In other words, he argued that it was not simply suggestion or transference love which overcame a patient's resistance to accepting the validity of his offered "anticipatory ideas." He argued that unless his interpretations (constructions) corresponded to actual *facts*, genuine insight concerning a patient's actual unconscious conflicts, which he believed a patient had to achieve as a prerequisite for therapeutic success, would not be achieved. Concerning charges that his patients might be led astray by his suggestions, late in his career Freud boldly proclaimed: "I can assert without boasting that such an abuse of 'suggestion' has never occurred in my practice" (Freud, 1937d, p. 262).

If a patient persisted in refusing to accept the correctness of his interpretations, either he would have to conclude that his interpretations were incorrect, or more likely blame this negative outcome on some inability of the patient to overcome their *resistance* and to successfully *work through* and *resolve transference issues* directed toward the analyst, as he believed happened in his treatment of "Dora" (see Freud 1905e, pp. 118–120)—although in this early case he accepted some blame for not properly recognizing the dynamics of "Dora's" transference toward him. Anne Salyard (1992) proposed that Freud's first conceptualization of transference developed during the early 1890s as he tried to understand how erotic issues complicated his hushed-up tragi-comic treatment of Emma Eckstein. She developed a severe infection and repeated profuse bleeding, which was almost fatal, as the result of a bungled nasal surgery he forced her to endure at the hands of his confidant Dr. Wilhelm Fliess, who convinced Freud that Emma's neurotic troubles were caused by issues related to the turbinal bones in her nose that needed correction. Information on the Emma case was at first found only in Freud's private letters to Fliess. Left out of the first expurgated collection of the letters published in 1950, it was revealed by Schur (1966, 1972) and later included in the complete letters (Masson, 1985). He callously blamed Emma's bleeding on her neurosis, exonerating Fliess (and himself) of responsibility (see March, 1895 letter, in Masson, 1985, pp. 116–118). See also Hartman (1983), Bonomi (2013), and Roudinesco (2016, pp. 58–59).

Toward the end of his career, Freud (1937c) had become pessimistic concerning the therapeutic efficacy of psychoanalysis. He now believed that the physiologically determined strength of the sexual drive, a constitutional factor, and the weakness of a patient's ego acquired in its defensive struggle to control the sexual drive, a psychological factor, could combine to make it impossible for a patient to overcome their resistance, thus making psychoanalysis an interminable process. By the late twentieth century, the view that psychoanalysis had become an interminable process had become a part of American popular culture, as epitomized by the films of Woody Allen. In the movie, *Annie Hall*, Annie asked Woody Allen's character if he saw an analyst. He replied that he had been in analysis for fifteen years and if he wasn't cured in one more year he would go to Lourdes.

Freud's psychoanalytic technique became defined by the methods of free association, interpretations of resistance, and the establishment of a transference toward the analyst with appropriate interpretation, working-through, and resolution. Psychoneurotic symptoms (defense neuroses) had to be traced back to earliest childhood. Since his evolving theories of childhood sexuality and the Oedipus complex attributed childhood sexual wishes to everyone, he developed the view that normal development required decisive repression and sublimation of such wishes in early childhood. After 1897, he developed the position that it was not the existence of such wishes, or repression, that was the cause of psychoneuroses, it was unsuccessful repression that was the cause with neurosis breaking out when repression failed and childhood sexual wishes reemerged in disguised form (compromise formations) as symptoms. Again, he never doubted that there were real cases of actual childhood sexual abuse. Traumatic memories and actual sexual abuse might play a role in some neuroses. However, post-1897, he no longer saw childhood sexual abuse and repressed memories of such abuse as *necessary preconditions* and causes for adult psychoneuroses. His primary focus became unresolved conflicts over childhood sexual wishes and fantasies and early autoerotic activities as the roots of adult psychoneuroses.

With the use of directed free association, patients were asked to talk about their dreams. As we have seen, by 1895 Freud had concluded that a dream was similar to a psychoneurotic symptom—they both were compromise formations. Since he believed that a dream was a symbolic disguised expression of conflicted wishes, psychoanalytic technique came to include the *interpretation* of dreams as "the royal road to a knowledge of the unconscious activities of the mind" (Freud, 1900a, p. 608).

CHAPTER 17

Childhood sexuality and evolutionary biology

In *Three Essays on the Theory of Sexuality* (1905d) and later revisions, Freud proposed and developed the concept of distinct pregenital stages of psychosexual development: oral, anal, phallic, and latency. During the first three stages, sexuality was expressed through particular erogenous zones, generating particular wishes for pleasure. The impact the child's pregenital experiences had on their evolving mental structure was seen by Freud as determining healthy, neurotic, or perverse adult characteristics.

At the start of *Three Essays on the Theory of Sexuality*, he stated that he expected that his readers already would be familiar with what he had to say concerning the "sexual aberrations." According to Freud (1905d): "The information contained in this first essay is derived from the well-known writings of Krafft-Ebing, Moll, Moebius, Havelock Ellis, Schrenk-Notzing, Löwenfeld, Eulenburg, Block and Hirshfeld ..." (p. 135n.). At the start of his discussion of "infantile sexuality" he acknowledged (1905d) that other authors had discussed precocious sexual activity in small children, but only as exceptional occurrences or as "horrifying instances of precocious depravity." However, as far as he knew "not a single author has clearly recognized the regular existence of a sexual instinct in childhood ..." (p. 173). Nevertheless, Adolf Baginsky, a prominent pediatrician in Berlin had written in 1901, "we find already in the child, in fully developed form, instincts [*Triebe*] and passions, conscious and unconscious deviations from what is morally correct, like the ones that we meet with uneasiness in the adults" (quoted by Bonomi, 1997, p. 50). Baginsky had been Freud's teacher on the subject of childhood neurology. After completing his studies with Charcot in 1886, he went to Berlin to receive training from Baginsky in pediatrics to prepare for the position at the Kassowitz Pediatric Institute in Vienna, which he occupied from 1886 to 1897 (Bonomi, 1994, 1997). He did not mention Baginsky in his survey of commentators on childhood sexuality at the start of his discussion of "infantile sexuality" (1905d, pp. 173–174n.).

In the oral stage of the first year, nursing and weaning were the areas in which Freud believed that control over pleasure-seeking activity regularly had to be achieved. According to him, the drive to reduce tension caused by the need for food and the drive to reduce sexual tension were originally both satisfied by the same activity directed toward the same object: sucking activity directed toward the mother. The reduction of drive tension rooted in the physiology of the body, achieved through mother-directed sucking activity, produced emotional attachments to the mother, and by extension, connections to other human caretakers.

In the anal stage of the second year, he believed that toilet training was the arena for conflict. The toddler had to learn how to compromise between expressing and inhibiting pleasure-seeking and aggressive impulses in order to minimize conflict with adult caretakers upon whom the child had become dependent for the meeting of emotional and physical needs.

In the phallic stage, starting about age three, he believed that the Oedipus complex, with autoerotic phallic stimulation, incestuous fantasies, aggressive impulses, and castration anxiety, was the primary conflict to be resolved (see Freud, 1905d, pp. 173–206). The Oedipus complex required a repression and a sublimation of sexual impulses and wishes directed toward the mother that first were established in the oral stage but now had become focused on the genital area, that is, on pleasure obtained through stimulation of the phallic erogenous zone. The child had to redirect sexual desire away from the original incestuous object, the mother, so that upon the achievement of puberty, genital sexual desire would not regressively turn backward toward the original incestuous object.

In *Three Essays on the Theory of Sexuality*, Freud first discussed the impact of anatomical distinctions on the development of boys and girls. Here, he introduced his concepts of a castration complex and penis envy. According to Freud (1905d), boys struggle over fear of castration resulting from observation of female anatomy, whereas girls "are overcome by envy for the penis—an envy culminating in the wish ... to be boys themselves" (p. 195). He developed the view that, for boys, the need to overcome the fear of castration by the father was the moving force behind the repression and sublimation of pregenital sexual wishes and identification with the father, which accomplished the resolution of the male Oedipus complex. For girls, on the other hand, he argued that a presumed belief that she already had been castrated made a clear-cut, final resolution of the Oedipus complex problematical. His evolving thoughts on the different male and female resolutions of the Oedipus complex will be discussed below in the discussion of development and adult character types.

With resolution of the Oedipus complex, around five to six years of age, the child entered the latency stage. This was a stage in which sexual impulses largely were redirected away from autoerotic practices, and away from the original incestuous object through sublimation—the substitution of socially acceptable objects and activities in place of forbidden objects and activities. The latency stage came to an end with the maturation of the genitals and the achievement of puberty.

Freud believed that failure to resolve any of the pregenital psychosexual conflicts created a fixation, an arrest of development in a pregenital stage which left an adult predisposed to regress to fixated pregenital modes of pleasure-seeking. Regressed sexuality might be acted out in "perversions" or expressed symbolically in psychoneurotic symptoms. According to Freud, a failure to resolve the Oedipus complex and a subsequent regression of the sexual instinct to incestuous object choice was a primary predisposition to adult psychoneuroses (see Freud, 1905d, pp. 231–243; and 1916–17, pp. 339–377). Psychoneurotic symptoms were symbolic (disguised, compromise formation) expressions of pregenital sexual impulses.

As we have seen in *The Interpretation of Dreams*, Freud (1900a) argued that it was only pregenital childhood sexual wishes that were subjected to repression and that were capable of revival during adult-hood as the motive force behind psychoneuroses. Back in 1897, after he told Fliess that he could no longer maintain his "seduction theory," he turned to certain concepts from evolutionary biology to reason why pregenital modes of sexual expression, in particular, were the targets of repression. He told Fliess in 1897:

> I have often had a suspicion that something organic plays a part in repression; … it was a question of the abandonment of for-mer sexual zones … I had been pleased at coming across a simi-lar idea in Moll. (Privately I concede priority in the idea to no one; in my case the notion was linked to the changed part played by sensations of smell: upright walking, nose raised from the ground, at the same time a number of formerly interesting sensa-tions attached to the earth becoming repulsive—by a process still unknown to me.) (In Masson, 1985, p. 279)

In *Three Essays on the Theory of Sexuality*, Freud (1905d) continued this theme when he stated that pregenital modes of sexual expression almost seemed "as though they were harking back to early animal forms of life" (p. 198).

In such speculations, he was guided by his belief in certain nineteenth-century biological theories. He believed in the validity of Haeckel's controversial "biogenetic law," the idea that the ontogenetic development of the individual recapitulated phylogenetic stages in the evolution of species (see Gould, 1977). Following Haeckel's law, he rea-soned that individual human development required the repression of earlier forms of sexual expression from our animal past that regularly and forcefully emerged in infancy and early childhood. The repression and sublimation of pregenital sexual impulses was a prerequisite for the final achievement of mature human mental and genital sexual organiza-tion (see Jackson, 1969; Sulloway, 1979, pp. 361–392; Ritvo, 1990).

In his preface to the 1915 third edition of *Three Essays on the Theory of Sexuality*, he argued: "The phylogenetic disposition can be seen at work behind the ontogenetic process" (p. 131). Throughout his post-1905 writings he continually relied on the idea that individual development recapitulated stages through which the ancestors of the human species passed in the progression into modern humankind. In his *Introductory Lectures on Psycho-Analysis*, Freud (1916–17) spoke of the development of the sexual instinct as a heritage, an

> abbreviated recapitulation of the development which all mankind has passed through from its primaeval days over long periods of time … this *phylogenetic* origin is, I venture to think, immediately obvious. Consider how in one class of animals the genital apparatus is brought in to the closest relation to the mouth, while in another it cannot be distinguished from the excretory apparatus … Among animals one can find, so to speak in petrified form, every species of perversion of the sexual organization. In the case of human beings … what is at bottom inherited is nevertheless freshly acquired in the development of the individual … (pp. 354–355)

In addition to his faith in Haeckel's "biogenetic law," he continuously maintained a strong faith in a controversial theory associated with Lamarck, the idea that acquired characteristics can be biologically transmitted to future generations. He reasoned that modern humans inherited characteristics that their ancestors acquired by behaving in a certain manner during the early history of the species. In *Totem and Taboo*, based upon ideas derived from Darwin's (1871) *The Descent of Man*, Freud (1912–13) argued that the original social organization of the human species was the primal horde, groups ruthlessly dominated by one male, the primal father. The primal father controlled all the women in the group, and only he could engage in sexual relations with them. Primal fathers drove maturing sons out of the group if the father perceived them as challenging his exclusive sexual rights. In a then-unpublished work, Freud (1915) even speculated that the primal father actually castrated his sexually mature sons (see Silverstein, 1989b).

As previously suggested by J. J. Atkinson in 1903, Freud (1912–13) argued that, finally, the sons who had been driven out banded together; they then returned and killed the primal father, thus gaining sexual access to the women of their primal horde. Stimulated by the writing of Robertson Smith, he also claimed (1912–13) that the rebelling sons devoured the slain father (see Freud, 1912–13, pp. 119–146, and

Wallace, 1983). Additionally, he (1912–13) contended that the sons were overwhelmed by guilt for the killing of the father and this guilt resulted in the renunciation of sexual relations with the women of their own group (incest), and the development of totemic religion in which symbols which represented the slain, devoured father became objects of worship. He located the beginnings of modern human social organization, morality, and religion in the killing of the primal father and the subsequent transformation of the paternally dominated horde into a community of brothers.

By combining Haeckel's and Lamark's ideas, he proposed that modern humans were predisposed to experience, concretely in childhood, the incestuous and parricidal wishes of the Oedipus complex, as well as castration anxiety. This was so, because in their individual development (ontogeny) they had to pass through a stage in which they concretely experienced inherited acquired impulses and fears that repeated and reflected actual incestuous, parricidal, and castrating activities carried out by primitive humans in primal hordes (phylogeny) (see Freud, 1912–13; 1916–17, pp. 358–377; Silverstein, 1986, 1989b).

Freud also used ideas derived from Haeckel and Lamark to explain the emergence of a moral force in human mental organization, the superego. This moral force evolved as an inheritance of a predisposition to achieve the repression of incestuous impulses and the redirection of parricidal impulses based upon characteristics acquired in human prehistory. Through experiencing and resolving the Oedipus complex, each child concretely repeated the experience of primal ancestors. In a footnote he added to *Three Essays on the Theory of Sexuality* (1905d) in 1920, he argued that "Every new arrival on this planet is faced by the task of mastering the Oedipus complex; anyone who fails to do so falls a victim to neuroses" (p. 226n.).

His (1912–13) anthropological speculations in *Totem and Taboo* were influenced by his readings of late-nineteenth- and early-twentieth-century cultural evolutionist theorists such as Herbert Spencer, Edward Tylor, James Frazer, J. J. Atkinson, and Robertson Smith, as well as his knowledge of the points of view of the nineteenth-century philosophers Ludwig Feurbach, Arthur Schopenhauer, and Friedrich Nietzsche (see Rieff, 1979; Wallace, 1983). He relied on his anthropological speculations to provide a biologically based evolutionary account for the origins and contemporary perpetuation of a universal sexual Oedipus complex. After 1911, he insisted that it was acceptance of the sexual nature of a universally experienced Oedipus complex that distinguished his view from the dissenting views being offered by Alfred Adler and Carl Jung. Because he began writing *Totem and Taboo* in 1911 to defend his sexual theory against the desexualizing approach he saw evolving in Jung's work, Freud, in 1911, could tell Jung that his interest in reading a great deal of anthropological writing was diminished "by the conviction that I am already in possession of the truths I am trying to prove" (in McGuire, 1974, p. 472).

Freud recognized that his anthropological speculations, created to explain why children had to concretely experience a sexualized Oedipus complex, constituted a myth of origins. Concerning his hypothesis of the origination of the Oedipus complex in an ontogenetic repetition of a phylogenetic inheritance that was traceable to the killing of the primal father, he stated (1921c): "To be sure, this is only a hypothesis, … a 'Just-So Story', as it was amusingly called by a not unkind English critic …" (p. 122). Here he was referring to *Just So Stories* published by Rudyard Kipling in 1902, a series of fairy tales for children crafted to explain the origins of such phenomena as: "How the Leopard Got His Spots" and "How the Camel Got His Hump."

Abram Kardiner (1977) recalled that, while he was in analysis with Freud, he was discussing the theory of primal parricide. Freud responded: "Oh, don't take that too seriously. That's something I dreamed up on a rainy Sunday afternoon" (p. 75). However, "if you did not take it seriously, your head would come off. I didn't know which way it was. 'Well,' he would say, 'this was just an idea'; but if you opposed him you got into serious trouble" (p. 75).

Even though Freud's hypothesis of the primal parricide has been vigorously rejected by cultural anthropologists, his theory of childhood incestuous wishes has been adopted by some cultural anthropologists to explain the existence of universal incest taboos. For example, see LaBarre (1958); Spiro (1982); also see Wallace (1983) and from psychology, see Lindzey (1967).

Freud (1912–13, pp. 153–154, and 1930a, p. 36) saw certain parallels between his hypothesis that all humans were born predisposed to experience concretely in individual development the incestuous and parricidal wishes acted out in human prehistory, and the Christian con-cept of original sin. He saw religion as claiming to redeem humanity from original sin, the sense of guilt that was common to everyone. How-ever, referring to his hypothesis of the killing of the primal father in pre-historic times as the historical antecedent of the universal sense of guilt, he argued (1930a), "we have been able to infer what the first occasion may have been on which this primal guilt, which was also the beginning of civilization, was acquired" (p. 136).

CHAPTER 18

Defending the sexual theory

In 1914, Freud was in an angry mood concerning challenges to his sexual theory put forth by former associates, Alfred Adler and C. G. Jung. He wrote "On Narcissism: An Introduction" in a state of rage (see Silverstein, 1986). In it he introduced a new division of instinctual drives: *ego libido* (self-love, self-preservation) versus *object libido* (other love, species preservation) and hoped to establish the fundamental *sexual* basis for human motivation. Adler was defining basic human motivation in nonsexual terms by emphasizing an aggressive "masculine protest" as the fundamental drive. Jung was rejecting Freud's vision of childhood sexuality, the sexual nature of the Oedipus complex, and the sexual etiology of all neuroses and schizophrenia. Freud was determined to defend his sexual theory by arguing that both sexual functions and self-preservative ego functions could be traced back to a common source of energy—the sexual libido (see Silverstein, 1986).

In 1907, Freud had told his new associate Carl Jung: "I could hope for no one better than yourself … to continue and complete my work" (in McGuire, 1974, p. 27). In 1908 he delegated a mission to Jung: "My selfish purpose, which I frankly confess, is to persuade you to continue and complete my work by applying to psychoses what I have begun with neuroses" (in McGuire, 1974, p. 168). He meant that Jung should apply his sexual (libido) theory to explain schizophrenia, a mission Jung never accepted as his own. Now, Freud (1914c) challenged Jung's nonsexual account of schizophrenia by arguing that in the early stages of development the same energy powered the sexual and ego drives (p. 76). Furthermore, he stated: "We are bound to suppose that a unity comparable to the ego cannot exist in the individual from the start; the ego has to be developed. The auto-erotic instincts, however, are there from the very first" (pp. 76–77). What we find in children, according to Freud (1914c), is an original direction of libido toward the self or ego. Gradually, some of his narcissistic libido becomes directed outward toward objects which are not part of one's self. Because there is a relatively fixed quantity of libido available to the individual at any particular moment, the more libido the individual directed toward objects, the less was invested in his own ego, and vice versa (p. 76). "Narcissistic libido" and "object libido" were thus inversely related. A phase of self-love in which one was self-absorbed and overestimated the importance of the self may be a normal feature of human development (p. 75). Contrary to Jung, Freud (1914c) now argued that schizophrenia had a libidinous base because the schizophrenic had regressed to an earlier state by directing toward his own ego the libido he had withdrawn from the external world (pp. 74–75).

Freud (1914c) also challenged Adler's motivational concept of the aggressive "masculine protest" by stating that if there is no unity "comparable to the ego" in the individual from the start, and if the development of the ego proceeds from "a differentiation of libido into a kind which is proper to the ego and one which is attached to objects" (p. 77), then Adler's "masculine protest" must be traceable to the threat of castration which injured the child's original sense of narcissistic well-being (p. 92). In addition, if the history of the development of the individual is inseparable from the dynamics of narcissism and libidinal conflict, then Freud's new conception of narcissism located the conflict within the ego itself, whereas Adler's "masculine protest" located the conflict between the ego and the other, presupposing the existence of an originally constituted unified ego which Freud was arguing against (Weber, 1982, p. 17). Up to this point in his theory-building, he used the term ego essentially as synonymous with self. With his creation of structural theory in 1923, as we have seen, the term ego was given a new specific meaning as one of the three hypothetical interactive mental agencies.

At the same time as he wrote "On Narcissism" (1914c) in a very aggressive mood, Freud also wrote the polemical "On the History of the Psycho-Analytic Movement" (1914d). Here he stated: "psycho-analysis is my creation ... no one can know better than I do what psycho-analysis is ..." (p. 7). He had two intentions in writing this treatise at this time: He wanted to take control of history by setting forth *his story* of the development of psychoanalysis as the *official history*, and he used this publication as a vehicle to present a blistering attack on the alternate approaches of Adler and Jung. In 1914, he wrote to Lou Andreas Salomé that he "intentionally gave everyone a good clobbering" (in Pfeiffer, 1972, p. 17).

Isidor Sadger, an early student, reported that Freud was not pleased if any of his students "insisted that he wanted to discover something on his own. Then he would become grumpy, yes, even angry ... For Freud was not merely the father of psychoanalysis but also its tyrant!" (2005, pp. 39–40).

According to Erich Fromm (1959),

> Freud was intolerant to those who questioned or criticized him in the least. To people who idolized him and never disagreed, he was kind and tolerant ... Freud was so dependent on unconditional affirmation and agreement by others, he was a loving father to submissive sons, and a stern, authoritarian one to those who dared to disagree. (p. 66)

We know that, because he had written "On Narcissism" (1914c) more because of the pressure of rival theorists' ideas than because of the pressure of facts, his zealous defense of sexual libido resulted in a weakening of his previous dualistic instinctual drive theory that had postulated a clear distinction between a driving force which was sexual and a restraining force that was not sexual, with qualitatively different energies at the roots of sexual and ego drives. Because it now appeared there was only one group of drives all energized by libido, Freud's core conception of psychic conflict, defense, and compromise still required a mental structure that was attuned to reality and that could oppose the sexual drive by means of its own source of energy. Therefore, it is not surprising that in 1914 he wrote to Karl Abraham: "Your acceptance of my 'Narcissism' affected me deeply ... I have a strong feeling of its serious inadequacy" (in H. C. Abraham & E. L. Freud, 1965, pp. 170–171). As previously discussed, recognition of the theoretical confusion he had created in 1914 required him to embark on later revisions in his conception of the instinctual drives, that is, the 1920 life versus death instincts.

Soon after, in 1915, Freud started writing a book containing a series of essays on his metapsychology, his psychology of unconscious mental processes. The completed book consisted of twelve essays. He never published the book, choosing to publish separately only five of the component metapsychological essays—three in 1915 and two in 1917 (see Silverstein, 1986, 1989b). In these essays, he continued to defend his sexual theory and he attempted to offer definitive statements on key components of his metapsychology, including instincts, repression, the unconscious, and dreams.

Before writing the metapsychological essays, he already had published *Totem and Taboo* (1912–13) in response to Jung's (1912) volume, *Transformations and Symbols of the Libido*, in which Jung argued that libido was not specifically sexual and the child had no actual sexual desire for the mother (see Wallace, 1983, pp. 105–108; and Silverstein, 1986). In *Totem and Taboo*, Freud went to war with Jung over the reality of childhood incestuous desires and the nature of a phylogenetic inheritance in the unconscious. As we have seen, Freud (1912–13) argued that humans were born predisposed to experience in their individual childhood-development (ontogeny) sexual and aggressive impulses that actually were acted out in human prehistory (phylogeny). He (1914c) had recast his motivational dualism in pan-sexual terms; ego libido versus object libido. Now, in 1915, Freud began writing twelve essays, still enraged over the challenges to his sexual theory coming from former associates, Adler and Jung (Silverstein, 1986, 1989b).

In 1915, Freud seriously maintained a superstitious belief that he was destined to die between the ages of sixty-one and sixty-two between May 1917 and May 1918 (see Silverstein, 1986, 1989b). In 1909, he told Jung:

> Some years ago I discovered within me the conviction that I would die between the ages of 61 and 62 … It made its appearance in 1899. At that time two events occurred. First I wrote *The Interpretation of Dreams* …, second I received a new telephone number, which I still have today: 14362 … In 1899 when I wrote *The Interpretation of Dreams* I was 43 years old. Thus, it was plausible

to suppose that the other figures signified the end of my life, hence 61 or 62. (in McGuire, 1974, p. 219)

The essays of 1915 were intended by Freud to be a *final theoretical testament* to defend his sexual theory, and to claim the title *psychoanalysis* for his views as opposed to those put forth by Adler and Jung.

He did not claim that the concepts he was presenting in 1915 were derived solely from his clinical observations. In his first essay, "Instincts and Their Vicissitudes," he stated (1915c),

> it is not possible to avoid applying certain abstract ideas to the material in hand, ideas derived from somewhere or other but certainly not from the new observations alone ... we come to an understanding about their meaning by making repeated references to the material of observation from which they appear to have been derived, but upon which, in fact, they have been imposed. (p. 117)

In his zeal to defend his sexual theory he wrote the twelve essays in great haste (Silverstein, 1986). He quickly published the essays: "Instincts and Their Vicissitudes" (1915c), "Repression" (1915d), and "The Unconscious" (1915e), because they were most critical for him in defining Freudian metapsychology and differentiating his views from the challenges of Adler and Jung. He held on to the rest because the defensive haste in which they were written left him unsatisfied with their contents.

Freud (1915c) used the essay "Instincts and Their Vicissitudes" to continue the defense of his sexual theory begun in *Totem and Taboo* and "On Narcissism." Here he made explicit the distinctly Freudian (as opposed to Adlerian or Jungian) conception of the function of the mind. For him, the mental apparatus served a biological purpose—the mastering of stimuli. The stimuli which most required mastering were those which emanated continually *from the interior of the body*—related to the *special chemistry of the sexual function*. The aim of mental functioning was to diminish the amount of excitement to which the organism was subjected (pp. 120–121, 124–125; see Silverstein, 1986).

He responded (1915c) to the challenge coming from Adler whom he saw proposing a special "aggressive instinct." Freud argued that all instincts were characterized by pressure—"the amount of force or the measure of the demand for work which it represents" (p. 122). Therefore, all instincts were aggressive in pursuing their aims, so it seemed pointless to isolate one conceptually self-contained aggressive instinct, as he believed Adler had done. As we have seen, later, in 1920, in *Beyond the Pleasure Principle*, he did elevate aggression to a primary force in human motivation, but as an expression of the death instinct.

Continuing to incorporate aggression into his conceptualization of the instincts related to the vicissitudes of libido, he (1915c) offered an analysis of the transformation of love into hate (p. 133). He did so to offer an example of how the "content" of an instinct might be changed into its opposite. He spoke of an aggressive, hating ego that was not simply the concomitant of childish egoism: "hating, too, originally characterized the relation of the ego to the alien external world ..." (p. 136), in response to unpleasurable stimuli. "Hate, as a relation to objects, is older than love ... it always remains in an intimate relation with the self-preservative instincts ..." (p. 139), as an expression of the pain reaction instigated by objects. In response to Adler, Freud (1915c) now allowed for some healthy innate aggressiveness in a manner consistent with his sexual theory and in contradistinction to his understanding of Adler's non-libidinal position (see Stepansky, 1977, p. 149). In "Mourning and Melancholia," which Freud published in 1917, he further emphasized an aggressive component of the ego instincts. He conceptualized how turning aggression, which originally had been directed toward a lost love object, back toward one's own ego, which now had incorporated the lost object to tolerate the loss, was a basis for pathological depression (to be discussed below).

In the essay, "Repression" (1915d) he stressed that the truly psychoanalytic view of the conflict inherent in mental life did not start with the struggle to be on top (Adler), or the struggle to individuate (Jung). The conflict at the heart of mental life was the struggle to deny the psychic representative of the sexual instinct entrance into consciousness when the resulting unpleasure would outweigh the possibility of pleasure (pp. 147, 151–153).

In the essay, "The Unconscious," he (1915e) expanded on the topographic point of view first published in 1900 in *The Interpretation of Dreams*. To contrast his views with those of Adler and Jung, Freud stressed that: "The nucleus of the Ucs consists of instinctual represen-tatives which seek to discharge their cathexis; that is to say, it consists of wishful impulses" (p. 186). He also described the different qualities attributed to psychic functioning according to whether the functioning was truly unconscious or merely preconscious (pp. 186–189). What was truly unconscious, or dynamically unconscious, was primary process wishful images experienced as reality. What was merely preconscious, or only descriptively unconscious, was secondary process, linguistically structured thought that was in the form required to make access to con-sciousness a possibility, if not necessarily a certainty.

In 1917, he published two more of the twelve essays: "A Metapsycho-logical Supplement to the Theory of Dreams" (1917d), and "Mourning and Melancholia" (1917e). In "Mourning and Melancholia" (1917e) he hypothesized that melancholia, or depression, was a reaction to the loss of an *ambivalently* loved person. The libido that had been directed toward the lost person was withdrawn into the ego that narcissistically incorporated the lost object to cope with the loss. The ego now harshly criticized itself as if it were the incorporated lost person, and the aggres-sion and hatred for the lost person became directed toward the self. In this manner, he explained the origin of melancholia and a depressed person's self-deprecation and sense of worthlessness.

In 1917, he appeared desirous of getting two more of the twelve essays on record in case he really did not survive his self-predicted death year (Silverstein, 1986). After he survived his predicted death year, his con-tinued dissatisfaction with the contents of the remaining essays and a more sober, clear-headed appraisal of the theoretical problems his exces-sive zeal in defending the sexual theory had created, persuaded Freud to abandon the remaining seven essays and to embark on a renewed period of theoretical creativity. His new lease on life motivated him to continue the struggle with Adler and Jung through his new theoretical develop-ments of the death instinct (1920g), structural theory (1923b), and a revised theory of anxiety (1926d).

For further commentary on Freud's struggles with Adler, Jung, and other colleagues, see Roazen (1975, 1992); Stepansky (1976, 1983); Steele (1982); Donn (1988); Groskurth (1991); Kerr (1993); and Rudnytsky (2011).

CHAPTER 19

Development of adult character types and neuroses

With the development of structural theory, Freud envisioned the ego developing through stages related to the emergence of the forms of the sexual instinct he had hypothesized in 1905, in *Three Essays on the Theory of Sexuality*. During each stage the ego had to gain control over sexual impulses, expressed through particular erogenous zones, and direct their expression in a manner that achieved harmony between instinctual demands and the restraints imposed by the external world. At each stage the ego developed a level of organization which it habitually employed in responding to a particular type of internal demand for sexual pleasure. At each stage the ego employed particular defense mechanisms that represented the level of maturity thus far achieved in the ego's development in response to the pressure of instinctual demands. If the ego experienced unusual difficulties in bringing instinctual impulses under control during any of the pregenital stages, a fixation was formed that determined a pattern or structure in the ego's organization which was brought forward to adulthood. A fixation in a level of ego development predisposed an adult to regress to modes of pleasure-seeking and tension-reduction characteristics of the developmental stage in which the fixation occurred

117

(a repetition compulsion); additionally, a fixation in a developmental stage left an adult predisposed to employ ego defense mechanisms characteristic of the stage in which the fixation occurred. The development of the ego's ability to master instinctual demands was the basis for adult character formation (Freud, 1923b, pp. 28–30).

In order to fully understand Freud's conception of adult character types and their relation to predispositions to differentiated adult psychoneuroses, a brief exploration of his varied ego defense mechanisms follows.

Starting with repression proper (secondary repression), the ego can engage in a number of pathogenic maneuvers to defend against anxiety caused by the pressure of primal repressed instinctual impulses and demands from the superego. Building upon her father's work in *Inhibitions, Symptoms and Anxiety* (1926d), Anna Freud outlined a number of pathogenic ego defenses described in various of her father's writings in her 1936 book, *The Ego and the Mechanisms of Defense* (see Fenichel, 1945, pp. 143–167). Some of Freud's conceptualized pathogenic ego defenses are listed below:

Repression proper: or secondary repression: the exclusion from consciousness of thoughts which arouse anxiety because they are closely associated with primal repressed unconscious wishes and impulses.

Denial: the prevention of the accurate cognizance of aspects of the real world associatively linked to unacceptable wishes or feelings; developing virtual "blind-spots."

Introjection: perceiving as belonging to one's self characteristics or traits which initially were perceived as belonging to, or part of, another person who was loved or feared.

Projection: the attribution to persons or objects of one's own unacceptable qualities, feelings, or wishes, and the perception that those wishes or feelings are directed by others toward oneself.

Reaction formation: the substitution of opposing feelings and impulses for one's unacceptable feelings and impulses so that, for example, "I hate you" is transformed into "I love you (to death)."

Displacement: the redirecting of associated energy from an unacceptable idea to a less anxiety-arousing idea which results in the idea which received the displaced energy becoming a significant focus of conscious attention; the unacceptable idea might remain in conscious-ness without apparent emotional impetus or significance.

Isolation: the separation of an unacceptable idea from the emotion orig-inally associated with that idea, and the severing of connections between the isolated idea and other connecting ideas. The isolated idea may remain conscious, but in an unemotional, separated-compartmentalized state.

Undoing: the performance of ritualized behaviors to drive away unacceptable thoughts or impulses.

Freud correlated adult character types with the functions of the erog-enous zones featured in the developmental stage in which a fixation occurred and the ego defense mechanisms correlated with the level of ego development associated with the fixated stage. He envisioned oral, anal, and phallic character types as casualties of unusually serious diffi-culties in ego development related to too much frustration, or too much indulgence, during a particular pregenital stage.

Freud's adult character types are:

The oral type: the oral character type experienced unusual difficul-ties associated with nursing and weaning, separation and loss. The oral character relied on the most primitive reality-distorting ego defenses: denial, introjection, and projection. The oral character displayed infan-tile traits such as: passive dependency or selfish grasping, poor judg-ment in trusting or mistrusting, and unreasonably hopeful expectations or pessimism.

The anal type: the anal character type experienced unusual diffi-culties in toilet training. The anal character relied on the primitive ego defenses: reaction formation, isolation, and undoing. The anal character manifested problems in impulse expression, or impulse control, such as: exaggerated cooperativeness or stubbornness, compulsive neatness or defiant messiness, and tight stinginess or loose overgenerosity (see Freud, 1908b).

The phallic type: the phallic character type experienced severe dif-ficulties in resolving the Oedipus complex. The phallic character relied on repression proper as an ego defense. The phallic character displayed childish traits such as: sexual promiscuity or rigid avoidance of sexual-ity, exhibitionistic self-presentation or attention avoidance, and prideful self-inflation or humble self-deprecation.

The genital type: the genital character type represented maturity in Freud's judgment. The genital character type passed through the pregenital stages without any unusual degree of difficulty or severe fixations. The genital character type accepted and expressed adult genital sexuality and could combine it with love for another person. The genital character employed sublimated libido for productive work.

If an adult developed a psychoneurosis, it was shaped by existing pregenital fixations and regression to the ego defenses associated with the stage of fixation. As a result, a fixation in the phallic stage associated with a failure to resolve the Oedipus complex predisposed an adult neurotic toward hysterical symptoms, while a fixation in the anal stage created a predisposition to obsessive compulsive neurosis. An oral fixation created a susceptibility to depression.

Freud saw resolution of the Oedipus complex as the prerequisite for the avoidance of a predisposition to adult psychoneuroses. After the development of structural theory and two decades after commenting on the psychological significance of anatomical distinctions between boys and girls in *Three Essays on the Theory of Sexuality* (1905d), he returned to this theme in earnest in relation to the resolution of the Oedipus complex. For both sexes, the Oedipus complex began as an intense desire for sole possession of the mother's love and the possibility of sexual pleasure through bodily contact with her. In boys, the desire for sexual pleasure became focused on the phallus, the penis. The boy developed a fear of castration from the father, his rival, and this castration anxiety motivated the boy to repress and sublimate taboo sexual wishes, and to identify with the feared father, identification with the aggressor. A boy's identification with the father created a strict, "follow-the-rules," demanding superego. Girls, on the other hand, according to Freud, believed that they already had been castrated so they could not identify with the father as the boy did (see Freud, 1924f, pp. 178–179; 1925j; 1931b; and 1933a, pp. 112–135). Instead, according to Freud, because "Anatomy is Destiny ..." (Freud, 1924f, p. 178), girls blamed their mothers for their perceived incomplete condition and turned toward fathers for love and compensation: "Her Oedipus complex culminates in a desire, which is long retained, to receive a baby from her father as a gift—to bear him a child" (Freud, 1924d, p. 179) "Thus the Oedipus complex escapes the fate which it meets with in boys: it may be slowly abandoned or dealt with by repression, or its effects may persist far into women's normal mental life" (Freud, 1925j, p. 257).

Girls identified with their mother out of fear of losing her nurturance. Because females did not identify with the father to ward off castration anxiety as boys did, Freud (1925j) stated: "I cannot evade the notion ... that for women the level of what is ethically normal is different from what it is in men. Their super-ego is never so inexorable, so impersonal, so independent of its emotional origins as we require it to be in men" (p. 257).

According to Freud (1930a):

> The work of civilization has become increasingly the business of men, it confronts them with ever more difficult tasks and compels them to carry out instinctual sublimations of which women are little capable. Since a man does not have unlimited quantities of psychical energy at his disposal, he has to accomplish his tasks by making an expedient distribution of his libido. (p. 103)

Did Freud really believe that he understood female psychology? Despite his pronouncements on the subject, he knew that he really did not understand the psychology of women very well. In his published pronouncements (1926e) he stated: "We know less about the sexual life of little girls than of boys. But we need not feel ashamed of this distinction; after all, the sexual life of adult women is a 'dark continent' for psychology" (p. 212). He once confessed to Marie Bonaparte: "The great question which has never been answered and which I have not yet been able to answer, despite my thirty years of research into the feminine soul, is '*Was will das Weib?*'" (What does the woman want?) (in Jones, 1955, p. 421).

For a review on Freud's writings on women, see Chodorow (1991), and Appignanesi and Forrester (1992, pp. 397–474), who also review the nature of Freud's relationships with significant women in his life.

CHAPTER 20

Freud on religion

W hat did Freud think about religious faith or religious practices as a path to human happiness? He argued (1907b and 1927c) that religion was an illusion comparable to an obsessional neurosis. He saw (1907b) parallels between ritualized obsessive actions in neurotic patients, and daily ceremonial rituals practiced by pious religious believers. He argued that both obsessive compulsive patients and pious followers of religious rituals suffered from an unconscious sense of guilt based upon only partially successful repression of instinctual impulses. In addition to repression, "a special *conscientiousness* is created which is directed against the instinct's aims; but this psychical reaction-formation feels insecure and constantly threatened by the instinct which is lurking in the unconscious" (p. 124). The forward pressure of the insecurely repressed impulses created unending conflict, as well as an unconscious sense of guilt, that was constantly being revived by new temptations to express the repressed impulses. This state of affairs, common in both obsessive compulsive neurotics and pious religious observers, produced "a lurking sense of expectant anxiety" and "an expectation of misfortune ... linked through the idea of punishment ..." (p. 123). The compulsive neurotic ritual, and the pious religious ritual, originated as an undoing defense mechanism, a protective behavior to ward off anxiety related to expectations of misfortune and punishment.

> The sense of guilt of obsessional neurotics finds its counterpart in the protestations of pious people that they know that at heart they are miserable sinners; and the pious observances (such as prayers, invocations, etc.) with which such people preface every daily act, and in especial every unusual undertaking, seem to have the value of defensive or protective measures. (pp. 123–124)

"A sense of guilt following upon continual temptation and an expectant anxiety in the form of fear of divine punishment have ... been familiar to us in the field of religion longer than in that of neurosis" (p. 125).

Freud (1927c and 1930a) traced the origin of the religious attitude to a regression to the infant's state of helpless dependence upon parents. When faced with powerful natural forces that could not be controlled, early humans transformed the power of nature into a transcendent cosmic father referred to as God. Freud (1930a) proclaimed: "I cannot think of any need in childhood as strong as the need for a father's protection ... The origin of the religious attitude can be traced back in clear outlines as far as the feelings of infantile helplessness" (p. 72). In his view,

> what the common man understands by his religion ... [is] the system of doctrines and promises which on the one hand explains to him the riddles of this world with enviable completeness, and, on the other, assures him that a careful Providence will watch over his life and will compensate him in a future existence for any frustration he suffers here. The common man cannot imagine this Providence otherwise than in the figure of an enormously exalted father. Only such a being can understand the needs of the children of men and be softened by their prayers and placated by the signs of their remorse. The whole thing is so patently infantile, so foreign to reality ... it is painful to think that the great majority of mortals will never be able to rise above this view of life. (p. 74)

Even though Freud (1927c, 1930a) traced the origin of the religious attitude back to a feeling of infantile helplessness, he again stressed how
individual development (ontogeny) recapitulated acquired behaviors
biologically inherited from human prehistory. He argued (1927c) that
"the primal father was the original image of God, the model on which
later generations have shaped the figure of God" (p. 42). Because "men
knew that they had disposed of their father by violence … in their reaction to that impious deed, they determined to respect his will thence-
forward" (p. 42). As he had argued in *Totem and Taboo* (1912–13, pp.
153–154), he (1930a) traced the origin of a universal human sense of guilt
to the killing of the primal father. This universal sense of guilt, comparable to the religious doctrine of original sin, was awakened in individual
development through the concrete experience of the sexual and parricidal impulses of the Oedipus complex, and the resultant development of
the superego that prohibited the expression of these pregenital impulses.
Harsh criticism from the superego caused the ego to experience guilt, or
moral anxiety that might be reduced through the formation of neurotic
symptoms; guilt also might be reduced through religious observance,
that is, placating God, the transcendent father figure through prayer as
well as through practicing defensive, undoing religious rituals.

In concluding that religion was based on regression to an infantile state of helplessness and a projective illusional dependency upon
a transcendent cosmic father who had to be obeyed and placated, and
in equating religious rituals with psychopathology, that is, with obsessive compulsive neurosis, Freud had been influenced by Feuerbach's
and Nietzsche's commentaries on religion. For background concerning
influences on Freud's development of his views on religion see: Küng
(1979); Rieff (1979); Wallace (1984); Stepansky (1986); Rizzuto (1998).

Final thoughts

We have seen that many of the ideas that became the building blocks of psychoanalytic theory were part of the powerful intellectual, scientific, and medical trends of the late nineteenth century: they were not derived solely from Freud's clinical data: they were imposed on them. He absorbed, synthesized, and applied ideas available from a variety of sources. Creatively, he succeeded in developing a new explanatory system for human behavior that is unrivaled in its comprehensiveness and its influence within psychology and the humanities. He also laid the foundation for the development of psychotherapy, talking cures. Through the volume of his publications and the theoretical brilliance with which he gave expression to his new system and method, he eclipsed his sources and created his own legend.

Late in his career in 1927, Freud reflected upon his achievements.

> After forty-one years of medical activity, my self-knowledge tells me that I have never really been a doctor in the proper sense ... the triumph of my life lies in my having, after a long and roundabout journey, found my way back to my earliest path ... In my youth I felt an overpowering need to understand something of

the riddles of the world in which we live and perhaps even con-
tribute something to their solution … I passed from the histology
of the nervous system, to neuropathology, and then … I began to
be concerned with the neuroses. I scarcely think, however, that
my lack of a genuine medical temperament had done much damage to my patients. (1926e, pp. 253–254)

Freud sought to solve the riddles of the neuroses and the riddles of the
human mind by using his psychoanalytic method as a research tool.
He hoped that therapeutic success with his patients would validate his
emerging causal hypotheses and theories. "It is only by carrying on our
analytic pastoral work," he declared, "that we can deepen our dawning
comprehension of the human mind. This prospect of scientific gain has
been the proudest and happiest feature of analytic work" (p. 256).

Freud confronted the dilemma inherent in the human mind taking
itself as an object for observation. He stated (1940a): "Every science is
based on observations and experiences arrived at through the medium
of our psychical apparatus. But since *our* science has as its subject that
apparatus itself, the analogy ends here" (p. 159). Even though he wanted
psychoanalysis to be viewed as a natural science, because the mind is
part of nature, he distinguished psychoanalysis from other natural sciences because its object of observation and its instrument for observing
were one and the same (see Forrester, 1997, pp. 240–248).

Freud created his metapsychology, his systematic mechanical models
of the mind, based upon analogies to the physical world, in his attempt
to be scientific in the broad *Naturwissenshaften* tradition within which
he understood the meaning of science. He saw his metapsychology as
a scientific contribution because it offered models to conceptualize the
nature of unobservable, unconscious lawful causal processes and contents that constitute psychic reality.

In his clinical practice Freud depended upon his ability to *interpret*
hidden meanings behind his patients' reported conscious thoughts,
associations, memories, and dreams. He saw his procedures as a scientific research tool to unlock secrets of the unconscious. However, he
often treated his inferences and interpretations as discovered "facts" that
his patients were obliged to accept as truth. But interpretations do not
meet an accepted standard for objective scientific data (Silverstein, 2003;

Borch-Jacobsen & Shamdasani, 2012). Subjective interpretations of the purpose, meaning, and significance of a person's thoughts, based upon particular hypothetical constructs concerning the basis and mechanics of mental functioning, cannot objectively be considered as proof for the validation of the truth value of the hypothetical constructs from which the interpretations were derived. Nevertheless, he believed that his "facts" supported his models of mental functioning and his diagnosis of his patients' maladies. He believed that his research method was comparable to the methods employed by physicists who made inferences about unobservable entities and forces, the true physical reality, based upon their empirical observations of the apparent physical world. He declared (1940a):

> We have discovered technical methods of filling up the gaps in the phenomena of our consciousness and we make use of these methods just as a physicist makes use of experiments. In this manner we infer a number of processes which are in themselves 'unknowable' and interpolate them in those that are conscious to us. (pp. 196–197)

Even though he located some intentional agencies in his mechanical mental apparatus, Freud tried to be scientific in the *Naturwissenschaften* tradition by conceptualizing the mind as a natural machine, and by conceptualizing general laws of human mental functioning. However, in his clinical work, where understanding the hidden intentions and meanings of a particular individual were a primary concern, his attempts to be scientific shifted between conceptualizing and applying general laws of mental functioning (*Naturwissenschaft*) and making subjective interpretations of a patient's personal intentions and meaning (*Geisteswissenschaft*). Freud saw his shifting between attempts at inferring unobservable lawful mental processes and inferring subjective personal meanings as dictated by the fact that, unlike any other phenomenon, the mind, as a natural phenomenon, could be investigated from both an objective and a subjective perspective.

In his clinical practice, as we have seen, it is clear that Freud often insisted that his patients had the responsibility to affirm the correctness of his interpretations of the hidden symbolic meanings of their symptoms and dreams and specific causes of their emotional difficulties. When patients accepted his interpretations and constructions, he saw their acceptance as scientific validation for his theories. On the other hand, when patients refused to accept his interpretations, he saw their behavior as validating his concepts of repression, resistance, sexual etiology, and improperly resolved transference. We know that once Freud was convinced that he had made correct inferences concerning a particular patient's behavior, he could be stubborn in refusing to accept a patient's unwillingness to accept them and accede to his authority.

Given the sometimes insensitive and callous treatment Freud displayed toward some patients, his aggressive and hateful treatment of some colleagues, his misrepresentations concerning some therapeutic outcomes, his sexism, and some of the arcane and anachronistic features of his metapsychology, he nevertheless left us with a set of ideas and concepts that have continuing relevance and application. A good example of such application is Anne Dailey's exploration of the relevance of Freud's dynamic unconscious to a critical examination of legal codes, interrogation techniques, and jurisprudence, in her *Law and the Unconscious: A Psychoanalytic Perspective* (2017).

In spite of his lack of scientific method, Freud created a significant scientific legacy in conceiving how dynamic unconscious processes, hidden wishes, conflicts, and intentions could affect cognitive functions such as perception, memory, and reasoning ability. See Westen (1998) for empirical support. In addition, he boldly confronted the issues of passion versus reason and how the propensity of the human mind for self-deception manifests itself in psychological defense mechanisms. He articulated in specific terms a human tendency to repeat in present adult relationships patterns established in childhood relations with parents, living in the present as if it were the past—repetition compulsions.

He focused on the fact that the subjective experience of our own body from within (feelings) is the core of our existence and confronted the mind–body problem by proposing the *dynamic unconscious mind* and its instinctual drives as the "missing link" between consciousness and the material body. Mark Solms (2015) documented convergence between these aspects of Freudian theory and emerging findings in neurological science. According to Nobel Prize-winning neural scientist,

Eric Kandel, "psychoanalysis still represents the most coherent and intellectually satisfying view of the mind" (1999, p. 505).

The issues of passion versus reason Freud focused on have been the perennial concerns of philosophers, poets, and playwrights. Perhaps that is why he often quoted imaginative writers such as Goethe, Heine, Schiller, and Shakespeare for their psychological insights, and why today his thinking remains most strongly embraced in the humanities.

We know that Freud's personal subjective approach to psychoanalysis is not science, and he had no interest in empirical testing of hypotheses derived from his theories because he believed it was not necessary; he already knew the truth. Nevertheless, for many years psychologists have carried out studies that subjected many hypotheses based upon Freudian concepts to empirical tests. Drew Westen (1998), assessing the literature on empirical tests of Freudian concepts, reported that a vast body of research in cognitive, developmental, personality and social psychology, supported a series of propositions derived from and central to Freud's theoretical structure. Among these are hypotheses concerning "unconscious cognitive, affective and motivational processes"; "the tendency for affective and motivational dynamics to operate in parallel and produce compromise solutions," and "the origins of many personality and social dispositions in childhood" (p. 333). Some of the best comprehensive reviews of this often overlooked data in search of an audience can be found in Masling (1983, 1987); Fisher and Greenberg (1977, 1978); Baron et al. (1992); Luborsky and Barrett (2006). The takeaway from this massive literature is that some of Freud's wide-ranging theoretical concepts received strong empirical support while others did not.

In contemporary clinical practice, Freudian perspectives can offer useful guidelines in providing ways of understanding the origins and dynamics of some neurotic behaviors; for example, see Kahr (2015). A review of major studies on the effectiveness of psychoanalytic treatment documents considerable evidence to support the efficacy of psychoanalytic-based therapies in helping those patients for whom it is an appropriate treatment (Galatzer-Levy et al., 2000). However, this is not to suggest that simply offering patients Freudian interpretations as explanations for the hidden meaning of their dreams and causes for their dysfunctional behaviors is an effective therapeutic procedure:

if the aim of psychoanalytic treatment is to help analysands move forward, simply telling them the hidden content won't help. Indeed, it may get in the way of genuine self-understanding … at the extreme, such words can be used as psychobabble: a phony "self-understanding" that is used to evade any real self-understanding. (Lear, 2005, p. 107)

Sometimes a cigar is just a cigar.

References

Abraham, H. C., & Freud, E. L. (Eds.) (1965). *A Psycho-Analytic Dialogue: The Letters of Sigmund Freud and Karl Abraham, 1907–1926*. New York: Basic Books.

Amacher, P. (1965). *Freud's Neurological Education and Its Influence on Psychoanalytic Theory*. New York: International Universities Press.

Andersson, O. (1962). *Studies in the Prehistory of Psychoanalysis*. Stockholm: Strenska Bökforlaget.

Appignanesi, L., & Forrester, J. (1992). *Freud's Women*. New York: Basic Books.

Baron, J. W., Eagle, M. N., & Wolitzky, D. L. (Eds.) (1992). *Interface of Psychoanalysis and Psychology*. Washington, DC: American Psychological Association.

Bergo, B. (2018). Sigmund Freud on Brain and Mind. In: S. Lapointe (Ed.), *Philosophy of Mind in the Nineteenth Century* (pp. 147–167). New York: Routledge.

Bernfeld, S. (1944). Freud's earliest theories and the school of Helmholtz. *Psychoanalytic Quarterly*, 13: 341–362.

Bernheim, H. (1887). *Suggestive Therapeutics: A Treatise on the Nature and Uses of Hypnotism*. New York: London Book Company, 1947.

Bettelheim, B. (1983). *Freud and Man's Soul*. New York: Alfred A. Knopf.

Billig, M. (2019). *More Examples, Less Theory: Historical Studies of Writing Psychology*. Cambridge: Cambridge University Press.

Boehlich, W. (Ed.) (1990). *The Letters of Sigmund Freud to Eduard Silberstein: 1871–1881*. Cambridge, MA: Harvard University Press.

Bonomi, C. (1994). Why have we ignored Freud the pediatrician? The influence of Freud's pediatric training for the origins of psychoanalysis. In: A. Haynal & E. Falzeder (Eds.), *100 Years of Psychoanalysis* (pp. 55–99). London: Karnac.

Bonomi, C. (1997). Freud and the discovery of infantile sexuality: a reassessment. In: T. Dufresne (Ed.), *Freud under Analysis* (pp. 35–51). Northvale, NJ: Jason Aronson.

Bonomi, C. (2013). Withstanding trauma: the significance of Emma Eckstein's circumcision to Freud's Irma dream. *Psychoanalytic Quarterly*, *82*: 689–740.

Borch-Jacobsen, M. (1996a). Neurotica: Freud and the seduction theory. *October*, *76*(Spring): 15–43.

Borch-Jacobsen, M. (1996b). *Remembering Anna O.: A Century of Mystification*. New York: Routledge.

Borch-Jacobsen, M., & Shamdasani, S. (2012). *The Freud Files: An Inquiry into the History of Psychoanalysis*. Cambridge: Cambridge University Press.

Boyer, J. W. (1978). Freud, marriage, and late Viennese liberalism: A commentary from 1905. *Journal of Modern History*, *50*: 73–102.

Brentano, F. (1874). *Psychology from an Empirical Standpoint*. London: Routledge & Kegan Paul, 1973.

Brown, N. O. (1959). *Life Against Death: The Psychoanalytic Meaning of History*. Middletown, CT: Wesleyan University Press.

Bunker, H. A. (1930). From Beard to Freud: a brief history of the concept of neurasthenia. *Medical Review of Reviews*, *36*: 108–114.

Byck, R. (Ed.) (1974). *Cocaine Papers by Sigmund Freud*. New York: Stonehill.

Carter, C. K. (1980). Germ theory, hysteria, and Freud's early work in psychopathology. *Medical History*, *24*: 159–274.

Carter, C. K. (1983). Infantile hysteria and infantile sexuality in late nineteenth century German language medical literature. *Medical History*, *27*: 186–196.

Castiglioni, A. (1958). *A History of Medicine*, 2nd edn. New York: Alfred A. Knopf.

Cavell, M. (1993). *The Psychoanalytic Mind: From Freud to Philosophy*. Cambridge, MA: Harvard University Press.

Charcot, J.-M. (1882–1885). *Clinical Lectures on Diseases of the Nervous System, Particularly on Hysteria*. R. Harris (Ed.). London: Tavistock/Routledge, 1991.

Chodorow, N. (1991). Freud on women. In: J. Neu (Ed.), *The Cambridge Companion to Freud* (pp. 224–248). Cambridge: Cambridge University Press.

Cohen, A. (2002). Franz Brentano, Freud's philosophical mentor. In: G. Van de Vijver & F. Geerardyn (Eds.), *The Pre-Psychoanalytic Writings of Sigmund Freud*. London: Karnac.

Cranefield, P. F. (1958). Josef Breuer's evaluation of his contribution to psychoanalysis. *International Journal of Psychoanalysis, 39*: 319–322.

Cranefield, P. F. (1966a). The philosophical and cultural interests of the Biophysics Movement of 1847. *Journal of the History of Medicine and Allied Sciences, 21*: 1–7.

Cranefield, P. F. (1966b). Freud and the "School of Helmholtz". *Gesnerus, 23*: 33–39.

Cranefield, P. F. (1970). Some problems in writing the history of psychoanalysis. In: G. Mora & J. L. Brand (Eds.), *Psychiatry and Its History* (pp. 44–55). Springfield, IL: Charles C. Thomas.

Cuddihy, J. M. (1974). *The Ordeal of Civility: Freud, Marx, Levi-Strauss, and the Jewish Struggle with Modernity*. New York: Dell.

Dailey, A. C. (2017). *Law and the Unconscious: A Psychoanalytic Perspective*. New Haven, CT: Yale University Press.

Dally, A. (2006). *Women Under the Knife: A History of Surgery*. Edison, NJ: Castle.

Donn, L. (1988). *Freud and Jung: Years of Friendship, Years of Loss*. New York: Charles Scribner's Sons.

Draenos, S. (1982). *Freud's Odyssey: Psychoanalysis and the End of Metaphysics*. New Haven, CT: Yale University Press.

Du Bois-Reymond, E. (1872). Über die Grenzen des Naturekennens. In: *Reden von Emil Du Bois-Reymond, Erster Band* (pp. 441–473). Leipzig, Germany: Verlag Von Veit, 1912.

Eissler, K. R. (2001). *Freud and the Seduction Theory: A Brief Love Affair*. Madison, CT: International Universities Press.

Elisha, P. (2011). *The Conscious Body: A Psychoanalytic Exploration of the Body in Therapy*. Washington, DC: American Psychological Association.

Ellenberger, H. (1970). *The Discovery of the Unconscious: The History and Evolution of Dynamic Psychiatry*. New York: Basic Books.

Ellenberger, H. (1972). The Story of "Anna O.": A critical review with new data. *Journal of the History of Behavioral Sciences*, 8: 267–279.

Ellenberger, H. (1973). Moritz Benedikt (1835–1920): An insufficiently appreciated pioneer of psychoanalysis. In: M. Micale (Ed.), *Beyond the Unconscious: Essays of Henri F. Ellenberger in the History of Psychiatry* (pp. 104–117). Princeton, NJ: Princeton University Press, 1993.

Ellis, H. (1910). Auto-eroticism (3rd edn.). In: *Studies in the Psychology of Sex, Vol. 1* (pp. 161–283). New York: Random House, 1936.

Erikson, E. H. (1964). The first psychoanalyst. In: *Insight and Responsibility* (pp. 19–46). New York: W. W. Norton.

Fenichel, O. (1945). *The Psychoanalytic Theory of Neurosis*. New York: W. W. Norton.

Ferenczi, S. (1933). Freud's influence on medicine. In: M. Balint (Ed.), *The Selected Papers of Sandor Ferenczi, M.D., Vol. 3* (pp. 143–155). New York: Basic Books, 1955.

Fisher, S., & Greenberg, R. P. (1977). *The Scientific Credibility of Freud's Theories and Therapy*. New York: Basic Books.

Fisher, S., & Greenberg, R. P. (Eds.) (1978). *The Scientific Evaluation of Freud's Theories and Therapy*. New York: Basic Books.

Forrest, D. (1999). *Hypnotism: A History*. London: Penguin.

Forrester, J. (1980). *Language and The Origins of Psychoanalysis*. New York: Columbia University Press.

Forrester, J. (1997). *Dispatches from the Freud Wars*. Cambridge, MA: Harvard University Press.

Frampton, M. F. (1991). Considerations on the role of Brentano's concept of intentionality in Freud's repudiation of the seduction theory. *International Review of Psycho-Analysis*, 18: 27–36.

Freud, A. (1936). *The Ego and the Mechanisms of Defense*. Revised edition. New York: W. W. Norton, 1966.

Freud, E. L. (Ed.) (1961). *Letters of Sigmund Freud: 1873–1939*. London: Hogarth.

Freud, S. (1884e). Über coca. In: R. Byck (Ed.), *Cocaine Papers by Sigmund Freud* (pp. 47–73). New York: Stonehill, 1974.

Freud, S. (1888). Gehirn [Brain]. In: A. Villaret (Ed.), *Handwörterbuch der Gesamten Medizin, Band 1* (pp. 684–697). Stuttgart, Germany: Ferdinand Enke.

Freud, S. (1888b). "Hysteria" and "hysteron-epilepsy". *S. E.*, *1*: 39–59. London: Hogarth.

Freud, S. (1890a). Psychical (or mental) treatment. *S. E.*, *7*: 280–302. London: Hogarth.

Freud, S. (1891b). *On Aphasia: A Critical Study*. London: Imago, 1953.

Freud, S. (1893c). Some points for a comparative study of organic and hysterical motor paralyses. *S. E.*, *1*: 157–172. London: Hogarth.

Freud, S. (1893f). Charcot. *S. E.*, *3*: 9–23. London: Hogarth.

Freud, S. (1894). The neuro-psychoses of defence. *S. E.*, *3*: 43–61. London: Hogarth.

Freud, S. (1895b). On the grounds for detaching a particular syndrome from neurasthenia under the description "anxiety neurosis". *S. E.*, *3*: 87–115. London: Hogarth.

Freud, S., & Breuer, J. (1895d). *Studies on Hysteria. S. E.*, *2*. London: Hogarth, 1955.

Freud, S. (1896a). Heredity and the aetiology of the neuroses. *S. E.*, *3*: 144–156. London: Hogarth.

Freud, S. (1896c). The aetiology of hysteria. *S. E.*, *3*: 189–221. London: Hogarth.

Freud, S. (1898a). Sexuality in the aetiology of the neuroses. *S. E.*, *3*: 261–285. London: Hogarth.

Freud, S. (1900a). *The Interpretation of Dreams. S. E.*, *4–5*: 1–625. London: Hogarth.

Freud, S. (1901b). *The Psychopathology of Everyday Life. S. E.*, *6*. London: Hogarth.

Freud, S. (1905c). *Jokes and Their Relation to the Unconscious. S. E.*, *8*. London: Hogarth.

Freud, S. (1905d). *Three Essays on the Theory of Sexuality. S. E.*, *7*: 130–243. London: Hogarth.

Freud, S. (1905e). Fragment of an analysis of a case of hysteria. *S. E.*, *7*: 3–122. London: Hogarth.

Freud, S. (1907b). Obsessive actions and religious practices. *S. E.*, *9*: 115–127. London: Hogarth.

Freud, S. (1908b). Character and anal erotism. *S. E.*, *9*: 168–175. London: Hogarth.

Freud, S. (1908d). "Civilized" sexual morality and modern nervous illness. *S. E.*, *9*: 179–204. London: Hogarth.

Freud, S. (1909d). Notes upon a case of obsessional neurosis. *S. E.*, *10*: 153–318. London: Hogarth.

Freud, S. (1910h). A special type of choice of object made by men. *S. E.*, *11*: 164–175. London: Hogarth.

Freud, S. (1910i). The psycho-analytic view of psychogenic disturbance of vision. *S. E.*, *11*: 211–218. London: Hogarth.

Freud, S. (1911b). Formulations on the two principles of mental functioning. *S. E.*, *12*: 215–226. London: Hogarth.

Freud, S. (1912d). On the universal tendency to debasement in the sphere of love. *S. E.*, *11*: 177–190. London: Hogarth.

Freud, S. (1912–13). *Totem and Taboo*. *S. E.*, *13*: 1–161. London: Hogarth.

Freud, S. (1914c). On narcissism: an introduction. *S. E.*, *14*: 67–102. London: Hogarth.

Freud, S. (1914d). On the history of the psycho-analytic movement. *S. E.*, *14*: 6–66. London: Hogarth.

Freud, S. (1915). *A Phylogenetic Fantasy: Overview of the Transference Neuroses*. I. Grubrich-Simitis (Ed.). Cambridge, MA: Harvard University Press, 1987.

Freud, S. (1915c). Instincts and their vicissitudes. *S. E.*, *14*: 111–140. London: Hogarth.

Freud, S. (1915d). Repression. *S. E.*, *14*: 143–158. London: Hogarth.

Freud, S. (1915e). The unconscious. *S. E.*, *14*: 161–215. London: Hogarth.

Freud, S. (1916–17). *Introductory Lectures on Psycho-Analysis*. *S. E.*, *15–16*: 9–496. London: Hogarth.

Freud, S. (1917d). A metapsychological supplement to the theory of dreams. *S. E.*, *14*: 217–235. London: Hogarth.

Freud, S. (1917e). Mourning and melancholia. *S. E.*, *14*: 239–258. London: Hogarth.

Freud, S. (1920g). *Beyond the Pleasure Principle*. *S. E.*, *18*: 3–143. London: Hogarth.

Freud, S. (1921c). *Group Psychology and the Analysis of the Ego. S. E.*, *18*: 67–143. London: Hogarth.

Freud, S. (1923b). *The Ego and the Id. S. E.*, *19*: 3–66. London: Hogarth.

Freud, S. (1924d). The dissolution of the Oedipus complex. *S. E.*, *19*: 172–179. London: Hogarth.

Freud, S. (1924f). A short account of psycho-analysis. *S. E.*, *19*: 191–209. London: Hogarth.

Freud, S. (1925d). *An Autobiographical Study. S. E.*, *20*: 7–74. London: Hogarth.

Freud, S. (1925j). Some psychical consequences of the anatomical distinction between the sexes. *S. E.*, *19*: 243–258. London: Hogarth.

Freud, S. (1926d). *Inhibitions, Symptoms and Anxiety. S. E.*, *20*: 77–174. London: Hogarth.

Freud, S. (1926e). *The Question of Lay Analysis. S. E.*, *20*: 179–258. London: Hogarth.

Freud, S. (1927c). *The Future of an Illusion. S. E.*, *21*: 3–56. London: Hogarth.

Freud, S. (1930a). *Civilization and Its Discontents. S. E.*, *21*: 59–154. London: Hogarth.

Freud, S. (1931b). Female sexuality. *S. E.*, *21*: 223–243. London: Hogarth.

Freud, S. (1933a). *New Introductory Lectures on Psycho-Analysis. S. E.*, *22*: 3–182. London: Hogarth.

Freud, S. (1937c). Analysis terminable and interminable. *S. E.*, *23*: 211–253 London: Hogarth.

Freud, S. (1937d). Constructions in analysis. *S. E.*, *23*: 255–269. London: Hogarth.

Freud, S. (1940a). *An Outline of Psycho-Analysis. S. E.*, *23*: 141–207. London: Hogarth.

Freud, S. (1940b). Some elementary lessons in psycho-analysis. *S. E.*, *23*: 279–286. London: Hogarth.

Freud, S. (1950a). Project for a scientific psychology. *S. E.*, *1*: 283–397. London: Hogarth.

Freud, S. (1956a). Report on my studies in Paris and Berlin, on a travelling bursary granted from the University Jubilee Fund, 1885–6. *S. E.*, *1*: 5–15. London: Hogarth.

Fromm, E. (1959). *Sigmund Freud's Mission: An Analysis of His Personality and Influence*. New York: Harper.

Fullinwider, S. P. (1983). Sigmund Freud, John Hughlings Jackson, and speech. *Journal of the History of Ideas*, *64*: 151–158.

Galatzer-Levy, R. M., Bachrach, H., Skolnikoff, A., & Waldron, S. (2000). *Does Psychoanalysis Work?* New Haven, CT: Yale University Press.

Gale, B. G. (2016). *Love in Vienna: The Sigmund Freud, Minna Bernays Affair*. Santa Barbara, CA: Praeger.

Gelfand, T. (1992). Sigmund-sur-Seine: fathers and brothers in Charcot's Paris. In: T. Gelfand & J. Kerr (Eds.), *Freud and the History of Psychoanalysis* (pp. 29–57). Hillsdale, NJ: Analytic Press.

Geeradyn, F. (1997). *Freud's Project: The Roots of Psychoanalysis*. London: Rebus.

Gill, M. M., & Holzman, P. S. (Eds.) (1976). *Psychology versus Metapsychology*. New York: International Universities Press.

Gilman, S. L. (1994). Sigmund Freud and the sexologists: a second reading. In: S. L. Gilman, J. Birmele, J. Geller, & V. D. Greenberg (Eds.), *Reading Freud's Reading* (pp. 47–76). New York: New York University Press.

Goldstein, R. G. (1995). The higher and lower in mental life: an essay on J. Hughlings Jackson and Freud. *Journal of the American Psychoanalytic Association, 43*: 495–515.

Gould, S. J. (1977). *Ontogeny and Phylogeny*. Cambridge, MA: Harvard University Press.

Gregory, F. (1977). *Scientific Materialism in Nineteenth Century Germany*. Dordrecht, the Netherlands: D. Reidel.

Grosskurth, P. (1991). *The Secret Ring: Freud's Inner Circle and the Politics of Psychoanalysis*. Reading, MA: Addison-Wesley.

Hale, N. G., Jr. (1971). *James Jackson Putnam and Psychoanalysis*. Cambridge, MA: Harvard University Press.

Harrington, A. (1987). *Medicine, Mind, and the Double Brain*. Princeton, NJ: Princeton University Press.

Hartman, F. R. (1983). A reappraisal of the Emma episode and the specimen dream. *Journal of the American Psychoanalytic Association, 31*: 555–585.

Hirschmüller, A. (1978). *The Life and Work of Josef Breuer: Physiology and Psychoanalysis*. New York: New York University Press.

Holt, R. (1989). *Freud Reappraised*. New York: Guilford.

Hughes, J. M. (1994). *From Freud's Consulting Room: The Unconscious in a Scientific Age*. Cambridge, MA: Harvard University Press.

Hughlings Jackson, J. (1875). On the anatomical and physiological localization of movements in the brain. In: J. Taylor (Ed.), *Selected Writings of John Hughlings Jackson, Vol. 1* (pp. 37–76). New York: Basic Books, 1958.

Hughlings Jackson, J. (1881). Remarks on dissolution of the nervous system as exemplified by certain post-epileptic conditions. In: J. Taylor (Ed.), *Selected Writings of John Hughlings Jackson, Vol. 2* (pp. 3–28). New York: Basic Books, 1958.

Hughlings Jackson, J. (1887). Remarks on evolution and dissolution of the nervous system. In: J. Taylor (Ed.), *Selected Writings of John Hughlings Jackson, Vol. 2* (pp. 76–118). New York: Basic Books, 1958.

Hughlings Jackson, J. (1890). On convulsive seizures. In: J. Taylor (Ed.), *Selected Writings of John Hughlings Jackson, Vol. 1* (pp. 412–457). New York: Basic Books, 1958.

Israëls, H., & Schatzman, M. (1993). The seduction theory. *History of Psychiatry,* *4*: 23–59.

Jackson, S. W. (1969). The history of Freud's concept of regression. *Journal of the American Psychoanalytic Association, 17*: 743–784.

Jones, E. (1953). *The Life and Work of Sigmund Freud, Vol. 1.* New York: Basic Books.

Jones, E. (1955). *The Life and Work of Sigmund Freud, Vol. 2.* New York: Basic Books.

Kahr, B. (2015). *Freud: Great Thinkers on Modern Life.* New York: Pegasus.

Kandel, E. R. (1999). Biology and the future of psychoanalysis: a new intellectual framework for psychiatry revisited. *American Journal of Psychiatry, 4*: 505–524.

Kandel, E. R. (2012). *The Age of Insight.* New York: Random House.

Kanzer, M. (1973). Two prevalent misconceptions about Freud's "Project" (1895). *Annual of Psychoanalysis, Vol. 1.* New York: Quadrangle, pp. 88–103.

Kardiner, A. (1977). *My Analysis with Freud.* New York: W. W. Norton.

Kern, S. (1973). Freud and the discovery of childhood sexuality. *History of Childhood Quarterly, 1*: 117–141.

Kern, S. (1975). The prehistory of Freud's dream theory: Freud's masterpiece anticipated. *History of Medicine, 6*: 83–92.

Kerr, J. (1993). *A Most Dangerous Method: The Story of Jung, Freud, and Sabina Spielrein.* New York: Alfred A. Knopf.

Klein, D. B. (1970). *A History of Scientific Psychology.* New York: Basic Books.

Klein, G. S. (1973). Two theories or one? *Bulletin of the Menninger Clinic, 37*: 102–132.

Klein, M. I. (1981). Freud's seduction theory: its implications for fantasy and memory in psychoanalytic theory. *Bulletin of the Menninger Clinic, 45*: 185–208.

Küng, H. (1979). *Freud and the Problem of God.* New Haven, CT: Yale University Press.

LaBarre, W. (1958). The influence of Freud on anthropology. *American Imago, 14*: 275–328.

Lear, J. (2005). *Freud,* 2nd edn. London: Routledge.

Levin, K. (1978). *Freud's Early Psychology of the Neuroses.* Pittsburgh, PA: University of Pittsburgh Press.

Libbrecht, K., & Quackelbeen, J. (1995). On the early history of male hysteria and psychic trauma: Charcot's influence on Freudian thought. *Journal of History of the Behavioral Sciences, 31*: 370–384.

Lindzey, G. (1967). Some remarks concerning incest, the incest taboo, and psychoanalytic theory. *American Psychologist, 22*: 1051–1059.

Luborsky, L., & Barrett, M. S. (2006). The history and empirical status of key psychoanalytic concepts. *Annual Review of Clinical Psychology, 2*: 1–19.

Macmillan, M. (1997). *Freud Evaluated—The Completed Arc.* Revised edition. Cambridge, MA: M.I.T. Press.

Maines, R. P. (1999). *The Technology of Orgasm: Hysteria, the Vibrator, and Womens' Sexual Satisfaction.* Baltimore, MD: Johns Hopkins University Press.

Makari, G. (1998). The seduction of history: sexual trauma in Freud's theory and historiography. *International Journal of Psychoanalysis, 79*: 857–869.

Makari, G. (2008). *Revolution in Mind: The Creation of Psychoanalysis.* New York: Harper Collins.

Masling, J. (Ed.) (1983, 1987). *Empirical Studies of Psychoanalytic Theories, Vols. 1 and 2.* Hillsdale NJ: Analytic Press.

Masson, J. F. (Ed.). (1985). *The Complete Letters of Sigmund Freud to Wilhelm Fliess: 1887–1904.* Cambridge, MA: Harvard University Press.

May, U. (1999). Freud's early clinical theory (1894–1896): outline and context. *International Journal of Psychoanalysis, 80*: 769–781.

McGrath, W. (1986). *Freud's Discovery of Psychoanalysis: The Politics of Hysteria.* Ithaca, NY: Cornell University Press.

McGuire, W. (Ed.) (1974). *The Freud/Jung Letters: The Correspondence Between Sigmund Freud and C. G. Jung.* Princeton, NJ: Princeton University Press.

McLaren, A. (1979). Contraception and its discontents: Sigmund Freud and birth control. *Journal of Social History, 12*: 513–529.

McLeod, M. N. (1992). The evolution of Freud's theory about dreaming. *Psychoanalytic Quarterly, 61*: 37–64.

Meissner, W. W. (2003). Mind, brain and self in psychoanalysis: II: Freud and the mind-body relationship. *Psychoanalysis and Contemporary Thought, 26*: 321–344.

Merlan, P. (1949). Brentano and Freud—a sequel. *Journal of the History of Ideas, 10*: 451.

Meynert, T. (1885). *Psychiatry.* New York: Hafner, 1968.

Micale, M. (1995). *Approaching Hysteria: Disease and Its Interpretations.* Princeton, NJ: Princeton University Press.

Nunberg, H., & Federn, E. (Eds.) (1975). *Minutes of the Vienna Psychoanalytic Society, Vol. 4.* New York: International Universities Press.

Oring, E. (1984). *The Jokes of Sigmund Freud*. Philadelphia, PA: University of Pennsylvania Press.

Orr-Andrawes, A. (1987). The case of Anna O: A neuropsychiatric perspective. *Journal of the American Psychoanalytic Association, 35*: 387–419.

Parisi, T. (1987). Why Freud failed: some implications for neurophysiology and sociobiology. *American Psychologist, 42*: 235–245.

Pfeiffer, E. (Ed.) (1972). *Sigmund Freud and Lou Andreas-Salomé: Letters*. New York: Harcourt Brace Jovanovich.

Phillips, A. (2014). *Becoming Freud: The Making of a Psychoanalyst*. New Haven, CT: Yale University Press.

Porter, R. (1993). The body and mind, the doctor and the patient: negotiating hysteria. In: S. L. Gilman, H. King, R. Porter, G. S. Rouseau, & E. Showalter. *Hysteria Beyond Freud* (pp. 225–285). Berkeley, CA: University of California Press.

Ramos, S. (2003). Revisiting Anna O: a case of chemical dependence. *History of Psychology, 6*: 239–250.

Rieff, P. (1979). *Freud: The Mind of the Moralist*. 3rd edn. Chicago, IL: University of Chicago Press.

Ritvo, L. B. (1990). *Darwin's Influence on Freud*. New Haven, CT: Yale University Press.

Rizzuto, A.-M. (1998). *Why Did Freud Reject God? A Psychodynamic Interpretation*. New Haven, CT: Yale University Press.

Roazen, P. (1975). *Freud and His Followers*. New York: DaCapo, 1992.

Roazen, P. (1992). The historiography of psychoanalysis. In: E. Timms & R. Robertson (Eds.), *Psychoanalysis in Its Cultural Context* (pp. 3–20). Edinburgh, UK: Edinburgh University Press.

Roazen, P. (1995). *How Freud Worked: First-Hand Accounts of Patients*. New York: Jason Aronson.

Rosenbaum, M., & Muroff, M. (Eds.) (1984). *Anna O. Fourteen Contemporary Reinterpretations*. New York: Free Press.

Roudinesco, E. (2016). *Freud in His Time and Ours*. Cambridge, MA: Harvard University Press.

Rudnytsky, P. L. (2011). *Rescuing Psychoanalysis from Freud*. London: Karnac.

Ruitenbeek, H. M. (1973). *Freud as We Knew Him*. Detroit, MI: Wayne St. University Press.

Rychlak, J. (1981). Freud's confrontation with the telic mind. *Journal of the History of the Behavioral Sciences, 17*: 176–183.

Sacks, O. (1998). The other road: Freud as a neurologist. In: M. S. Roth (Ed.), *Freud: Conflict and Culture* (pp. 221–234). New York: Alfred A. Knopf.

Sadger, I. (2005). *Recollecting Freud*. [Trans. by J. M. Jacobsen & A. Dundes of *Sigmund Freud: Persönliche Erinnerungen* (1930).] Madison, WI: University of Wisconsin Press.

Salyard, A. (1992). Freud's narrow escape and the discovery of transference. *Psychoanalytic Psychology*, 9: 347–367.

Salyard, A. (1994). On not knowing what you know: object-coercive doubting and Freud's announcement of the seduction theory. *Psychoanalytic Review*, 81: 659–676.

Sand, R. (1988). Early nineteenth century anticipation of Freudian theory. *International Review of Psycho-Analysis*, 15: 465–479.

Sand, R. (1992). Pre-Freudian discovery of dream meaning: the achievements of Charcot, Janet and Krafft-Ebbing. In: T. Gelfand & J. Kerr (Eds.), *Freud and the History of Psychoanalysis* (pp. 215–229). Hillsdale, NJ: Analytic Press.

Schimek, J. (1987). Fact and fantasy in the seduction theory: a historical review. *Journal of the American Psychoanalytic Association*, 35: 937–965.

Schrenck-Notzing, A. (1892). *The Use of Hypnosis in Psychopathia Sexualis*. (1895 English Translation.) Philadelphia, PA: F. A. Davis.

Schur, M. (1966). Some additional "day residues" of the "specimen dream" of psychoanalysis. In: R. M. Loewenstein, L. M. Newman, M. Schur, & A. J. Solnit (Eds.), *Psychoanalysis—a General Psychology* (pp. 45–85). New York: International Universities Press.

Schur, M. (1972). *Freud Living and Dying*. New York: International Universities Press.

Silverstein, B. R. (1985). Freud's psychology and its organic foundation: sexuality and mind-body interactionism. *Psychoanalytic Review*, 72: 203–228.

Silverstein, B. R. (1986). "Now comes a sad story": Freud's lost metapsychological papers. In: P. E. Stepansky (Ed.), *Freud: Appraisals and Reappraisals: Contributions to Freud Studies, Vol. 1* (pp. 143–195). Hillsdale, NJ: Analytic Press.

Silverstein, B. R. (1988). Will the real Freud stand up, please? *American Psychologist*, 43: 662–663.

Silverstein, B. R. (1989a). Freud's dualistic mind-body interactionism: Implications for the development of his psychology. *Psychological Reports*, 64: 1091–1097.

Silverstein, B. R. (1989b). Oedipal politics and scientific creativity: Freud's phylogenetic fantasy. *Psychoanalytic Review, 76*: 403–424.

Silverstein, B. R. (1997). A follow-up note on Freud's mind-body dualism: what Ferenczi learned from Freud. *Psychological Reports, 80*: 369–370.

Silverstein, B. R. (2002). Psychoanalysis: origins and history. In: E. Erwin (Ed.), *The Freud Encyclopedia* (pp. 435–444). New York: Routledge.

Silverstein, B. R. (2003). *What was Freud Thinking? A Short Historical Introduction to Freud's Theories and Therapies*. Dubuque, IA: Kendall/Hunt.

Silverstein, B. R. (2007). What happens in Maloja stays in Maloja: inference and evidence in the "Minna Wars." *American Imago, 64*: 283–289.

Silverstein, S. M. (1988). A study of religious conversion in North America. *Genetic Psychology Monographs, 114* (3): 261–305.

Silverstein, S. M., & Silverstein, B. R. (1990). Freud and hypnosis: the development of an interactionist perspective. *The Annual of Psychoanalysis, Vol. 18.* Hillsdale, NJ: Analytic Press, pp. 175–194.

Skues, R. A. (2006). *Sigmund Freud and the History of Anna O.: Reopening a Closed Case*. London: Palgrave Macmillan.

Solms, M. (2002). An introduction to the neuroscientific works of Sigmund Freud. In: G. Van De Vijver & F. Geerardyn (Eds.), *The Pre-Psychoanalytic Writings of Sigmund Freud* (pp. 17–35). London: Karnac.

Solms, M. (2015). *The Feeling Brain: Selected Papers on Neuropsychoanalysis.* London: Karnac.

Solms, M., & Saling, M. (1986). On psychoanalysis and neuroscience: Freud's attitude to the localizationist tradition. *International Journal of Psychoanalysis, 67*: 397–416.

Solms, M., & Saling, M. (1990). *A Moment of Transition: Two Neuroscientific Articles by Sigmund Freud*. London: Karnac.

Sotelo, C. (2020). The history of the synapse. *Anatomical Record, 303*: 1252–1279.

Spiro, M. (1982). *Oedipus in the Trobriands*. Chicago, IL: University of Chicago Press.

Steele, R. S. (1982). *Freud & Jung: Conflicts of Interpretation*. London: Routledge & Kegan Paul.

Stepansky, P. E. (1976). The empiricist as rebel: Jung, Freud, and the burdens of discipleship. *Journal of the History of Behavioral Sciences, 12*: 216–239.

Stepansky, P. E. (1977). *A History of Aggression in Freud*. New York: International Universities Press.

Stepansky, P. E. (1983). *In Freud's Shadow: Adler in Context*. Hillsdale, NJ: Analytic Press.

Stepansky, P. E. (1986). Feuerbach and Jung as religious critics—with a note on Freud's psychology of religion. In: P. E. Stepansky (Ed.), *Freud: Appraisals and Reappraisals* (pp. 215–239). Hillsdale, NJ: Analytic Press.

Stewart, W. A. (1967). *Psychoanalysis: The First Ten Years, 1888–1898*. New York: Macmillan.

Sugarman, S. (2016). *What Freud Really Meant: A Chronological Reconstruction of His Theory of the Mind*. Cambridge: Cambridge University Press.

Sulloway, F. (1979). *Freud: Biologist of the Mind: Beyond the Psychoanalytic Legend*. New York: Basic Books.

Sulloway, F. (1992). Reassessing Freud's case histories: the social construction of psychoanalysis. In: T. Gelfand & J. Kerr (Eds.), *Freud and the History of Psychoanalysis* (pp. 153–192). Hillsdale, NJ: Analytic Press.

Swales, P. J. (1982a). Freud, Minna Bernays and the conquest of Rome; new light on the origins of psychoanalysis. *New American Review, 1*: 1–23.

Swales, P. J. (1982b). Freud, Johan Weier and the status of seduction: the role of the witch in the conception of fantasy. In: L. Spurling (Ed.), *Sigmund Freud: Critical Assessments, Vol. 1* (pp. 330–358). London: Routledge, 1989.

Swales, P. (1983a). Freud, Krafft-Ebing, and the witches: the role of Krafft-Ebing in Freud's flight into fantasy. In: L. Spurling (Ed.), *Sigmund Freud: Critical Assessments, Vol. 1* (pp. 359–365). London: Routledge: 1989.

Swales, P. J. (1983b). Freud, cocaine, and sexual chemistry, the role of cocaine in Freud's conception of the libido. In: L. Spurling (Ed.), *Sigmund Freud: Critical Assessments, Vol. 1* (pp. 273–301). London: Routledge, 1989.

Swales, P. J. (1986). Freud, his teacher and the birth of psychoanalysis. In: P. E. Stepansky (Ed.), *Freud: Appraisals and Reappraisals: Contributions to the Freud Studies, Vol. 1* (pp. 3–82). Hillsdale, NJ: Analytic Press.

Swales, P. J. (1995). Once a cigar, always a cigar. Review of R. Webster, *Why Freud was Wrong: Sin, Science, and Psychoanalysis*. *Nature, 378* (2 November): 107–108.

Swales, P. J. (2003). Freud, death and sexual pleasures: on the psychical mechanism of Dr. Sigm. Freud. *Arc de Cercle: An International Journal of the History of the Mind Sciences, 1*: 5–74.

Tauber, A. I. (2010). *Freud: The Reluctant Philosopher*. Princeton, NJ: Princeton University Press.

Wallace, E. R. (1983). *Freud and Anthropology: A History and Reappraisal.* New York: International Universities Press.

Wallace, E. R. (1984). Freud and religion: A history and reappraisal. *The Psychoanalytic Study of Society, Vol. 10.* Hillsdale, NJ: Analytic Press, pp. 113–161.

Weber, S. (1982). *The Legend of Freud.* Minneapolis, MN: University of Minnesota Press.

Westen, D. (1998). The scientific legacy of Sigmund Freud: towards a psychodynamically informed psychological science. *Psychological Bulletin, 124*: 333–371.

Whitebook, J. (2017). *Freud: An Intellectual Biography.* Cambridge: Cambridge University Press.

Zentner, M. R. (2002). Nineteenth-century precursors of Freud. In: E. Erwin (Ed.), *The Freud Encyclopedia* (pp. 370–383). New York: Routledge.

Index